AMERICAN ADVENTURES
TRUE STORIES FROM AMERICA'S PAST

1870 to Present

By
Morrie Greenberg

**Former English-Social Studies Consultant,
Los Angeles Unified School District**

Brooke-Richards Press
Northridge, California

OTHER BOOKS BY MORRIE GREENBERG
The Buck Stops Here, A Biography of Harry Truman, Macmillan
We the People (multi-state history text adoptions, including California), D.C. Heath
Adventures in United States History (Federal Grant)
Survival in the Square, Brooke-Richards Press
American Adventures, Brooke-Richards Press

Published by
Brooke-Richards Press
9420 Reseda Blvd., Suite 511
Northridge, California 91324

Printed in the United States of America

Library of Congress Cataloging-in-Publication Data
Greenberg, Morrie.
    American adventures: true stories from America's past / Morrie Greenberg.
        p. cm.
    Contents: pt 2. 1870-Present
    Summary: A kaleidoscope of fifteen stories about United States history.
    1. United States—History—Anecdotes—Juvenile literature.
[1. United States—History.] I. Title.
E178.3.G82   1990   973   90-2652

ISBN 0-9622652-2-5

Contents

Acknowledgments

The author wishes to acknowledge the fine input provided by these teachers: Matthew Cruz, Diane Goldstein, Dr. Helen Lodge, John Plevack, George Rollins, Sue Shapiro, Ron Sima, and Richard Tibbits.

Book design by Suzette Mahr. Production assistance, Rand Self. Editor Audrey Bricker.

About the Author

Morrie Greenberg has taught at Juvenile Hall School (elementary and secondary), Foshay Middle School, Sequoia Middle School, Le Conte Middle School, Bouquet Canyon Boys' School, and Jefferson Adult School — all in the Los Angeles area. He has served as a social studies department chairperson, an administrative consultant, and a middle school principal. As English-Social Studies consultant for the Los Angeles Unified School District, he worked with, and offered suggestions to, teachers at thirty different middle schools. He also taught Methods of Teaching Social Studies at California State University, Northridge, and coordinated a tutoring program for teenagers there. He is presently supervising student teachers at CSUN.

To The Reader

This is a book of stories that other young readers and listeners have found interesting and exciting. We hope you will too.

To the left of each story is a timeline and a box titled "What Else Was Happening?" This will give you an idea of what was happening at about the same time the story is taking place. Since the stories and timelines follow in order, you will get a chance to see how our nation has grown.

Though the stories in *American Adventures* happened long ago, you will discover that many people and events in the stories remind you of what is happening today. A writer in ancient Rome had something to say about this over 2,000 years ago. He wrote:

**Why do you laugh? Change but
the name and the story is told of you.**

The idea was a simple one: Why not make learning about American history a story-telling adventure with each story breathing life and meaning into America's past? The result of this idea was *American Adventures, True Stories From America's Past, 1770 to 1870.*

Since the publication of the first part of *American Adventures,* so many students, parents, and teachers have pointed out that they found *American Adventures* a wonderful way to learn about history, it seemed only natural to follow with *American Adventures, Part 2.* We believe you will find these stories just as exciting, and just as inspiring.

1872

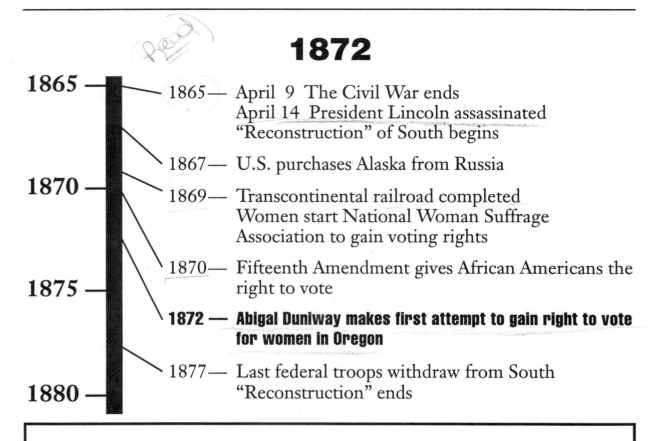

1865 —

1870 —

1875 —

1880 —

1865— April 9 The Civil War ends
April 14 President Lincoln assassinated
"Reconstruction" of South begins

1867— U.S. purchases Alaska from Russia

1869— Transcontinental railroad completed
Women start National Woman Suffrage
Association to gain voting rights

1870— Fifteenth Amendment gives African Americans the
right to vote

**1872 — Abigal Duniway makes first attempt to gain right to vote
for women in Oregon**

1877— Last federal troops withdraw from South
"Reconstruction" ends

What Else Was Happening?

President Abraham Lincoln did not want to punish the Southerners for leaving the Union. He wanted the Southern states back in the Union quickly. "With malice (hate) towards none, with charity (forgiveness) for all," he said. Lincoln set up the "Freedmen's" (freed men's) Bureau to help the freed slaves. After Abraham Lincoln was assassinated in 1865, President Andrew Johnson tried to carry on Lincoln's ideas.

Congress would not let Johnson carry out his ideas for "Reconstruction." Instead, Congress saw to it that troops were stationed in most of the Southern states. Former Southern soldiers and leaders could not take part in voting or running the government. On the other hand, the Fifteenth Amendment gave African Americans the right to vote for the first time (though women still could not vote). Seven Southern states sent African American representatives to Congress. In time, however, Northerners lost interest in the South; they wanted to concentrate on their own problems. In 1877 all the troops were taken out of the Southern states, and Reconstruction ended.

#1

The Woman Who Dared

"**Y**our husband—he's been hurt in an accident."

Abigail's eyes grew large and welled up with tears as her neighbor, standing outside the doorway, described what had happened.

"He was hauling a load of hay," she began. "The horses—they whirled around so fast the wagon tipped over," Abigail rushed out the door as her neighbor shouted after her. "—and one of the wheels rolled right over Ben."

Ever since Ben Duniway and Abigail had married eleven years before, life—so it seemed—had been one struggle after another. Farming in the Oregon Territory in the 1850's had not been easy. Ben had tried to earn a living on one farm after another. When he ran out of money, he sold his farm and took to hauling goods for other farmers. After all, with five "young ones" at home he had to make a living.

And now the accident!

Later that day, with Ben resting in bed, Abigail gave thanks that he was alive. However, the accident had crippled her cheerful, hard-working husband. He would no longer be able to do the kind of work that brought food to the family.

What was Abigail going to do now? Abigal Duniway was no stranger to tough times. When she was seventeen, her father sold his farm in Missouri and the family set out for Oregon. For six terrible months, the family moved westward in a covered wagon, braving dust storms, snow flurries, and fierce desert heat. On the journey Abigal watched both her mother and brother grow ill and die. Twenty-four hundred miles from Missouri, an older toughened Abigal—filled with hope for a new and better life—reached the Oregon Territory. A year later, in 1853, she married Ben.

Like most husbands of that day Ben Duniway had always told his wife not to be concerned about money. Now, Abigail would have to be the "breadwinner" and find a way to support the family. She rented the attic of her home to a few young women and agreed to teach them reading and writing. This gave her a chance to earn some money. A year later, Abigail and Ben moved to Albany, Oregon. Here Abigail opened a shop for ladies' hats with the money she had saved. The ladies who came to Abigail's shop often stayed long enough to chat. They talked of many things—how to get the children to behave, what to cook, what to sew. But more often than not, they talked about their husbands. Abigail listened and began to hear things that bothered her. The women worked as hard, even harder, than their husbands; yet they had no say about how the family money was spent.

In these early days, whatever a man or woman earned belonged to the man. The man owned all the family's property. A man had the right to leave his wife and children and

The years went by, and each time, Abigil said, "We will just try again."

take away everything the family owned. If he wanted to, he could take the children too. Many women customers told Abigail how they had to beg their husbands for money if they wanted to buy something for themselves or the children. Some of the men, so it seemed to Abigail, treated grown women who had children as if they were children themselves.

One evening, Abigail sat eating dinner with her husband, complaining how unfair she thought all of this was. Why couldn't a woman own property? Why couldn't she go to court and sue someone? Why did all the laws favor men?

Ben Duniway listened politely before he answered. "The laws are one-sided," he said, "because men make the laws. And as long as other men vote for the men who make the laws, the laws will always be one-sided."

Abigail looked up from her dinner. *Of course!* She had expected a complicated explanation, but the answer was simple. As long as women can not vote, men will keep right on making laws that keep all the rights for men. Abigail made up her mind: no matter how difficult it was, no matter how long it took, she would fight to see that women were given the right to vote. She realized the fight would take time, but not even Abigail could have guessed how long and difficult the struggle would be.

Abigail started a weekly newspaper. The newspaper had some news, but most of the stories and articles were written by Abigail to get people to think about the way women were treated. She was spreading the word, first in Oregon, and then in Washington and Idaho. Soon, she was going on speaking trips, urging the public to "wake up!"

These trips were not pleasant. People did not want her speaking in their churches or in the town lecture halls on such "outrageous" subjects as a woman's right to vote. And so, when Abigail arrived in a new town, she had to look for a home or a barn or a beat-up old building—or even the back of a saloon—as a place to speak. No matter where she appeared, some men in the audience tried to ridicule, or make fun of her. This did not bother Abigail. After letting a "heckler" have his say, Abigail bounced back with a smart remark or two of her own.

"Is your mother a lunatic, or an idiot, or a criminal?" Abigal would ask.

"She certainly is not," a man would shout back indignantly.

"Well," Abigail would politely explain, "None of the people I mentioned can vote— and neither can your mother."

Abigail was careful not to appear mean or unpleasant when she said these things. After all, she wanted to win the men in the audience to her way of thinking. Even so, she became very adept at dodging the rotten eggs and old fruit her unhappy listeners hurled at her.

It took years, but Abigail began winning more and more people to her way of thinking. In 1872, a bill was started in Oregon's state legislature that would allow women to vote. Abigail spoke before this group of men who made the laws for Oregon, but the bill did not pass. Abigail's answer to this failure was a simple one: we will just try again.

And try again she did—two years later. When that effort failed, a "referendum" election was held. A "referendum" is an election where the citizens themselves vote on whether or not to pass a law. When the referendum failed, Abigail had the same answer—we will just try again. Years went by, and more elections were held, but each election failed to win the right to vote for women, and each time Abigail said: we will just try again. Finally, an election to give women the right to vote was held again in Oregon in 1912. By now, Abigail was a gray haired old woman of seventy eight—but still as full of fight as ever. For 40 years she had battled for the right to vote. When Abigail was asked what she would do if this election also failed, she proudly announced: "Why, I'll just try again."

This time, however, the voters gave women the right to vote in Oregon. There would be no need to try again. Abigail Duniway was honored all over the West as the "Grand Old Woman" of women's rights. Oregon had become the ninth state to give women the right to vote. Eight years later, in August, 1920, the Nineteenth Amendment to the Constitution was passed. At last, women in every state had the right to vote—thanks to the work done by pioneers like Abigail Duniway.

Writing/Journal Activities

TAKE IT OR LEAVE IT

Here are eight words. Copy out the four words that describe Abigail Duniway the best.

1. intelligent   2. inspiring   3. belligerent   4. boring

5. persistent   6. resolute   7. dull   8. weak

2. SEARCH AND FIND

Find the word (or words) closest to the meaning of the underlined word in each sentence. Then copy the sentence using that word (or words) in place of the underlined word.

1. Abigail opened a <u>millinery</u> store.
   shoe   hat   glove   dress

2. People thought her speech was <u>outrageous</u>.
   flattering   courteous   well done   disgraceful

3. Some men <u>ridiculed</u> her.
   made fun of   ignored   hurt   offended

4. Men in the audience were <u>heckling</u>.
   teasing   laughing   throwing things   staring

5. She became <u>adept</u> at dodging things thrown at her.
   bad   awkward   embarrassed   good

6. Abigail spoke before the Oregon <u>legislature</u>.
   lawmakers   police officers   governor   school board

3. ANSWER BACK

If you were Abigail Duniway, how would you answer someone who said this to you:

1. "Why do you want women to have the right to vote?"

2. "Why are you nice to people who are rude to you?"

3. "Don't you know when it's time to give up?"

Let's Talk—Discussion Activities

4. THINK IT THROUGH

Give as many answers as you can for each question.

—Why do you think men did not want to give women the right to vote for such a long time?

—When is it a good idea to be persistent (to keep on trying)? When is it a bad idea?

5. TAKE A SIDE

Here are two opinions on the same subject. Take one side or the other, and then give all the reasons you can for the side you take.

—"Women should have the right to vote, but they should not be allowed to work at certain jobs."

—"Women can take on any of the jobs a man can do."

Cooperative Group Activities

6. IMAGINE

Imagine that you were given the task of writing a constitution for a new democratic country. Be able to explain or justify the answers you give. Would you allow someone to vote who—

1. has been in prison?
2. can not read or write?
3. is visiting from another country?
4. was born in another country, but has become a citizen?
5. is only 16 years old, but is very intelligent?
6. is 18 years old, but has very poor school grades?
7. has a foreign accent?
8. does not believe in democracy?

7. A LOOK BACK

Select one of the events shown on the timeline for this story. Use other books or articles to gather more information about the event, and try to find out why the event was important. Present the information to the class or group.

1874

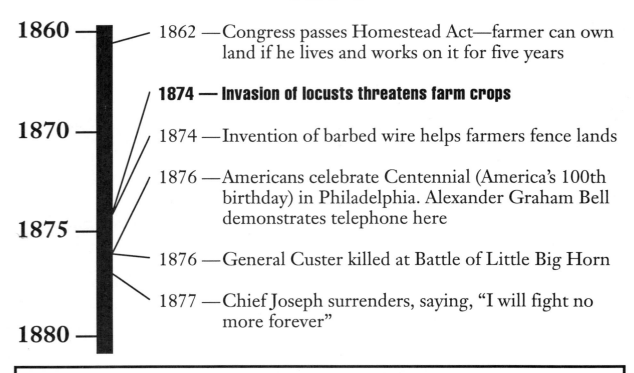

1860 —

1862 —Congress passes Homestead Act—farmer can own land if he lives and works on it for five years

1874 — Invasion of locusts threatens farm crops

1870 —

1874 —Invention of barbed wire helps farmers fence lands

1876 —Americans celebrate Centennial (America's 100th birthday) in Philadelphia. Alexander Graham Bell demonstrates telephone here

1875 —

1876 —General Custer killed at Battle of Little Big Horn

1877 —Chief Joseph surrenders, saying, "I will fight no more forever"

1880 —

What Else Was Happening?

Early Americans did not settle on the flat land east of the Rocky Mountains known as the Great Plains; they believed this land was just a large desert. After the Civil War, however, the U.S. government forced the Indians off their lands on the Plains, and opened the area up to settlers. American settlers were soon grazing cattle and raising sheep on the Plains, and farmers began homesteading plots of land.

Most Americans still made their living by farming, but by the 1870's this was changing. Because the railroads could ship so much raw materials to factories, more and more workers were needed to work in different industries. As more Americans began working in factories, the small towns nearby grew larger. Some grew into cities. Most Americans still lived on farms and in small towns in the 1870's, but, as each year went by, more of them were moving to the cities.

#2
The Mysterious Cloud

Head down, the gray-haired farmer hoed the soil around the corn with strong, steady, strokes. As he broke through the rich Kansas soil, he smiled in satisfaction this warm spring morning in 1874. It looked like another good crop. Suddenly, the farmer eased his grip on the hoe, letting it slip noiselessly to the ground. *Something's wrong*, he thought. *Something's terribly wrong*.

A giant shadow was moving across the land—across the farmhouse, the barn, the whole field. *No cloud moved like that!* The farmer looked up. Using his left hand to shield his eyes, he squinted nervously towards the horizon. A huge, dark cloud was spreading in all directions, blotting out more and more of the sky. In a matter of moments, the dark cloud covered the whole sky. At the same time, a strange whirring, buzzing sound grew louder and louder until it sounded like the roar of a waterfall.

Something hit the farmer's arms, his cheeks, his legs, his chest. The old farmer muttered an oath, then grabbed his hoe and began swinging it wildly at the air, then the ground, then back at the air. While flailing away with the hoe—and between gasps for air—the farmer shouted to his two sons who were working in the barn. "Come out! Bring your shovels. The locusts are here!"

Yes, indeed, the locusts had arrived.

Scenes like what happened on this Kansas farm were repeated on farmlands across the Great Plains throughout the spring and summer of 1874. From the Rocky Mountains in the west to the Mississippi River on the east, these pesky locusts—more commonly known as grasshoppers—attacked America's farmlands. Like a giant invading army, millions and millions of locusts landed in one place and began a march of destruction. The march was slow—usually less than ten feet a minute—but the huge blanket of chewing, chomping, chattering locusts moved over everything and anything. One such army was 100 miles wide and at least a half mile high!

Nothing escaped them. Corn, wheat, cotton, potatoes, tree leaves, tree bark—every crop that lay in the path of the moving army disappeared. Underground crops were not safe either. Gaping holes showed where onions, carrots, or turnips had been growing. And if the locusts ran out of food, they attacked clothing, or wooden farm tool handles, or leather. Locusts did not attack animals or people, but they could eat the harness on a horse, or the clothing left on a line to dry.

It usually took two to three days before the locusts moved on. By then, the land looked as though a fire had scorched it bare. No part of the Great Plains was safe. In the summer, the locusts grew wings, and drifted in the breeze, blackening the sky as they traveled hundreds of miles to new places. Once they landed, nothing seemed to stand in the way. Not hills, not mountains, not valleys. And, if they came to a stream, millions of them crawled one upon the other until they created a "bridge" of drowned locusts that the others could scramble over.

The results were devastating. From the Rocky mountains to the Mississippi, from Canada to Texas, they spread their destruction. The farmers were like soldiers furiously trying to defend their lands against an invading army. They stomped, crushed, burned, smothered, sprayed, or drowned their enemy. They attacked them with large, flat shovels. They shot at them with guns, rang bells, and clanged pots and pans. They wrapped oil soaked rags around a wire, set the rags on fire, and then moved the wires along the locust covered ground. They sprayed them with kerosene, set prairie fires, trampled them with cattle. They dug ditches, and used specially designed machines pulled by horses called,

The huge blanket of chomping, chattering locusts moved over everything, and anything.

"Hoppercatchers," or "Hopperdozers." They had long rollers that turned and crushed the locusts, or they carried fire and scorched them. Some machines used huge fans that sucked and smashed the locusts.

Nothing really worked. There was no way to stop an army made up of millions of locusts that stretched for miles in all directions. Winter weather finally ended the locust horror in 1874. Now, the farmers wondered, was it over?

The melting snows of spring in 1875 brought the answer—another invasion as bad as the one in 1874. For four years, from 1874 to 1877, the invasions continued through spring and summer. Then, as winter drew near in 1877, some farmers thought they noticed something different. *Weren't the locusts acting sluggish? Didn't they seem to be moving slower? Was this a sign that they were dying off?*

As mysteriously as they had arrived, the locusts disappeared in 1877. They never appeared again in such large numbers. Why? Perhaps it was because of a change in the weather; no one knows for certain. We do know that years before the invasion of the 1870's, early explorers and early settlers described locust invasions, but never in the numbers that came from 1874 to 1877.

The most amazing part of the story is not the invading locust, but the American farmer. A few farmers gave up and headed east, but most of them remained on their farms—just as they had done so many times before. Despite blizzards, tornadoes, forest fires, scorching droughts, and yes, locust invasions, American farmers stayed on their land. They worked hard, took whatever nature threw at them, and—always optimistic—waited for better times.

Writing/Journal Activities

1. TAKE IT OR LEAVE IT

Here are eight words. Copy out the four words that best describe the farmers in this story.

1. struggling   2. cheerful   3. dogged   4. persevering

5. pleased   6. rested   7. contented 8. determined

2. SEARCH AND FIND

Find the word (or words) closest to the meaning of the underlined word in each sentence. Then copy the sentence using that word (or words) in place of the underlined word.

1. The <u>chomping</u> locusts moved slowly.

   traveling   chewing   wiggling   squirming

2. The land looked <u>scorched</u>.

   frozen   burnt   deserted   barren

3. The farmers were <u>devastated</u> by what they saw.

   hurt   confused   puzzled   overwhelmed

4. Despite winter <u>blizzards</u> the farmers stayed on their land.

   snow storms   rains   currents   breezes

5. <u>Gaping</u> holes showed where the plants had been growing.

   wide open   small   tiny   shallow

6. Everyone agreed that the locust invasion was a <u>catastrophe</u>.

   calamity   bad accident misfortune   hardship

3. ANSWER BACK

If you were a farmer in this story, how would you answer someone who said this to you:

1. "Why don't you give up and get a job in a factory?"

2. "What's so difficult about being a farmer?"

3. "What do your young children do on the farm?"

Let's Talk—Discussion Activities

4. THINK IT THROUGH

Give as many answers as you can for each question.

—Why did the farmers stay on their land and keep on farming no matter how bad conditions got?

—Why are farmers able to produce so much more food today than they did 100 years ago?

5. TAKE A SIDE

Here are two opinions on the same subject. Take one side or the other, and then give all the reasons you can for the side you take.

—"It is much better for a family to live in a city than on a farm or small town."

—"No—it is much better for a family to live on a farm or in a small town."

Cooperative Group Activities

6. IMAGINE

1. Imagine you farmed during the 1870's. Describe three or more calamities that forced you to give up farming.

2. Imagine you have a farm today with modern farm equipment. Explain to a farmer of the 1870's how different farming is today.

3. Imagine you were a farmer in the 1870's. Pick the four most important important qualities you think a farmer should have? There are no "right" or "wrong" answers, but be able to justify or explain your answers.

persistent   patient   healthy   aggressive
caring   industrious   logical   dependable

7. A LOOK BACK

Select one of the events shown on the timeline for this story. Use other books or articles to gather more information about the event, and try to find out why the event was important. Present the information to the class or group.

1889

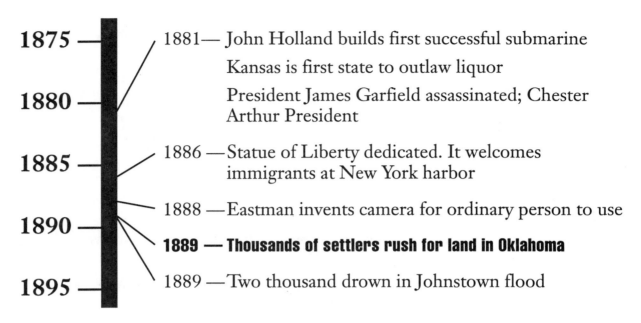

1875 —

1880 —

1881 — John Holland builds first successful submarine

Kansas is first state to outlaw liquor

President James Garfield assassinated; Chester Arthur President

1885 —

1886 — Statue of Liberty dedicated. It welcomes immigrants at New York harbor

1890 —

1888 — Eastman invents camera for ordinary person to use

1889 — Thousands of settlers rush for land in Oklahoma

1895 —

1889 — Two thousand drown in Johnstown flood

What Else Was Happening?

Americans had always moved west to settle the frontier, but the Oklahoma land rush of 1889 appeared to mark the end of the western frontier. Thanks to new inventions and natural resources, America was becoming an industrial nation. Workers were needed to work in factories and mines. During the 1880's more than 5 million people came to America. Almost all of them were poor. They came in "steerage," where people sat huddled and cramped closely together below deck, in stale air. Though some of the immigrants moved to farms, most of them settled in the cities where new industries and factories had opened.

America's early immigrants came from western European countries, mainly from Great Britain and Germany. A few came from south of the border. All of this changed in the 1880's. Millions of immigrants poured in from southern and eastern Europe—mainly from Italy, Russia, and Poland. Americans seemed willing to let these newer immigrants find their place in America.

#3

The Oklahoma Land Rush

Moments before twelve noon, on April 22, 1889, the U.S. soldiers stationed along the winding border of the Oklahoma Indian Territory, pulled their pistols from their holsters, pointed them skyward—and waited. At exactly twelve noon, they fired into the air. The resounding boom of the guns was the signal for thousands upon thousands of men, women, and children—some on foot, some on horseback, some in carts or buggies, some even aboard trains—to scramble across the Oklahoma border.

The strangest race in American history had begun!

The reason for the race went back to the early days of American pioneering. The United States government had signed treaties with the Indian tribes who lived in Oklahoma. Under the treaties, Oklahoma was to be Indian Territory for "as long as grass grows and water flows." The Indians allowed a few Americans to raise cattle in the Territory, and a few railroads were built there, but Americans could not settle on the land.

During the 1840's and 1850's, more and more Americans went west and began to settle the land all around Oklahoma. Here they plowed the fertile land, planted trees and crops, built log cabins, and made homes of sod. After the Civil War ended in 1865, many more pioneers moved west. They settled in Texas, Kansas, Arkansas, and Missouri—but never, because of the treaties with the Indians, in neighboring Oklahoma.

By the 1880's, good farm land was getting harder and harder to find. Some Americans looked with longing at the empty stretches of land in the Oklahoma Indian Territory, and wondered why they could not settle there. Oklahoma stood out like an island—surrounded as it was by the farms and towns of neighboring states. A few of these Americans—they were called "Boomers"—decided to break the law and move into the Indian territory. U.S. Army troops quickly forced these "Boomers" off the land, and threatened to put them in jail if they returned.

The "Boomers" however, claimed that it would only be a matter of time before the Indian Territory would be opened for settlement. The "Boomers" turned out to be right. By 1889, the U.S. government had forced the Indian tribes to sell their rights to the land. On March 23, 1889, President Benjamin Harrison declared that a part of the Oklahoma Indian Territory would be open to settlement in exactly 30 days. Each of the thousands of 160 acre lots of land—surveyed earlier by the government—would go to the first man to get to the lot and claim it. The man claiming it had to be 21 years old, the head of a family, and own no more than 160 acres of land.

The Oklahoma settlers waited anxiously for the race to begin.

There was one catch, however: No one could go into the Territory before noon on April 22, and anyone who was caught in the Territory before this time, would lose all rights to claim any land.

President Harrison's announcement hit the people in the U.S. who did not own land like a bolt of lightening. At last, a chance to work a farm, to own a home! All over the country, people hungry for land said their quick good-byes, and headed for the Oklahoma border. They came from every state in the Union—on foot, on horseback, in two-wheeled carts, and in covered wagons with signs nailed on that read, "Oklahoma or Bust," or "Bound for Home." Piled high atop the wagons and carts were food, bedding, pots, pans, tables, chairs, and every kind of farm equipment. Some brought supplies for opening grocery stores, saloons, blacksmith shops, or carpenter shops.

As April 22 drew near, fifty thousand men, women, and children camped along the border and waited. In the distance lay the promise of a new life, but for now they could only gaze at the green grass and winding streams. Many of the men who waited had left their families behind, planning to send for them if they made a claim. Others had come with their families, but hoped to race ahead and

have wives and children catch up later. A few old time "Boomers" had waited as long as ten years. The government had stationed troops all along the border to make certain there would be no problems. Most of the settlers waited patiently for the signal to begin, but the soldiers found a few men—called "Sooners"—hiding along streams in the woods inside the Territory and hauled the cheaters off.

The excitement reached its peak when the "great day" arrived. Some settlers planned to board trains that ran into the Territory. They clamored aboard the railroad cars like an army of ants, and when a car filled up, climbed on the roof or clung to the windows. In fairness to those going by horse or wagon, the train engineers had been ordered to move the trains slowly.

When the guns sounded at twelve noon, a thundering clatter was heard and great clouds of dust rose to the sky. Wagons, buggies, carts, trains, and people on foot and on horseback rushed into the Oklahoma Territory. As the creaking wagons twisted and turned for the best positions, the men on horseback galloped past. The race was on!

When a man reached a plot of land he wished to claim, he drove a stake with his name painted on it into the ground. Then he waved his hat wildly as a signal to others that the land was his. Not every settler was this lucky. One pioneer concentrated so hard on his running that he did not see the water well some soldiers had dug a few weeks before. He fell in, and, despite his cries for help, the people rushed right by him. No one wanted to stop and risk getting behind the others. Another time, a half-dozen men and a woman rushed towards a choice lot. The men had no way of knowing that the "woman" was really a sneaky young man in a dress. They graciously gave the claim to the "woman."

Some anxious men jumped off before the trains came to a stop, tumbling head over heels along the ground. Those that managed to get up limped along as best they could, heading towards a claim. Sometimes, two or more settlers claimed the same piece of land. This lead to yelling or fist-fighting, and even some shooting. Most of the settlers, however, were good-natured and went by the rules.

Once a settler picked a lot, he had 60 days to file his claim in a land office, and six months to move his family on the land. Even then, the land was not really his. The settler had to stay on the land and work—or "homestead" it—for five years. Only at the end of the five years, was the settler given a deed that said the land belonged to him.

Because there were less than 12,000 lots available for this first Oklahoma land rush, many of the 50,000 people had to return to their homes tired and disappointed. A good part of the Oklahoma Territory was still available, however, and soon more land rushes were held—one in 1891, another in 1892, and the biggest land rush of all, in 1893. The race in 1893 attracted over 100,000 people. There were so many arguments and fights however, the government turned to lotteries to give out the rest of Oklahoma's land. The lottery worked better, but old timers loved to recall the "good old days" when men raced each other across the prairie in search of a home.

The race was on!

Courtesy, The Bettmann Archive

Writing/Journal Activities

1. TAKE IT OR LEAVE IT

Here are eight scenes an artist might have painted. Copy out the four scenes the artist might include in a painting of the Oklahoma land rush.

1. galloping horses
2. pans of gold
3. overloaded carts
4. men fist fighting
5. women dancing
6. a signed treaty
7. a large building
8. a quiet schoolroom

2. SEARCH AND FIND

Find the word (or words) closest to the meaning of the underlined word in each sentence. Then copy the sentence using that word (or words) in place of the underlined word.

1. At the sound of the guns, the buggies <u>scrambled</u> across the line.
   hurried   creaked   squeaked   rolled

2. The Indians had a <u>treaty</u> with the U.S. government.
   misunderstanding   spoken agreement
   signed agreement   long conversation

3. The <u>creaking</u> wagons raced on.
   noisy   old   broken   shattered

4. The settlers <u>concentrated</u> as they raced.
   wandered about   thought hard   avoided accidents   fought sleep

5. The settler <u>filed a claim</u> in an office.
   claimed citizenship   claimed he was wronged
   claimed he could vote   claimed the land

6. A settler <u>homesteaded</u> on the land in order to own it some day.
   built a barn   planted crops   lived and worked   raised cattle

3. ANSWER BACK

If you were an Oklahoma settler, how would you answer someone who said this to you:

1. "Why are you going to all this trouble for a piece of land?"

2. "What do you think of the men who cheated and tried to get into Oklahoma before the gun sounded?"

Let's Talk — Discussion Activities

4. THINK IT THROUGH

Give as many answers as you can for each question.

—In this story the government gave away land. Sometimes, the government makes an owner sell his or her land to the government to build a road, a school, a fire station, or other things. Do you think this is right? Explain.

5. TAKE A SIDE

Here are two opinions on the same subject. Take one side or the other, and then give all the reasons you can for the side you take.

—"The U.S. government was wrong in pushing the Indians off their lands."

—"The Indians were not making good use of the land. Settlers could develop the land. The government did the right thing."

Cooperative Group Activities

6. IMAGINE

Imagine you are in the Oklahoma land rush. Decide if each of these places are good or bad locations to stake your claim for a farm. (Some locations might be both good and bad.) Explain your answers.

1. near roads	2. near a lake	3. near a swamp
4. near a river	5. near a desert	6. near a railroad line
7. near neighbors	8. near a trading center	9. on low land

Imagine you are in the Oklahoma land rush. Decide which of these you would take with you. Explain your answers. There are no "right" or "wrong" answers, but be able to justify or explain your answers.

1. a map of Oklahoma or a dog	2. a frying pan or a wheelbarrow
3. books or wooden stakes	4. hammer and nails or furniture
5. oxen or horses	6. money or pots and pans

8. A LOOK BACK

Select one of the events shown on the timeline for this story. Use other books or articles to gather more information about the event, and try to find out why the event was important. Present the information to the class or group.

1890

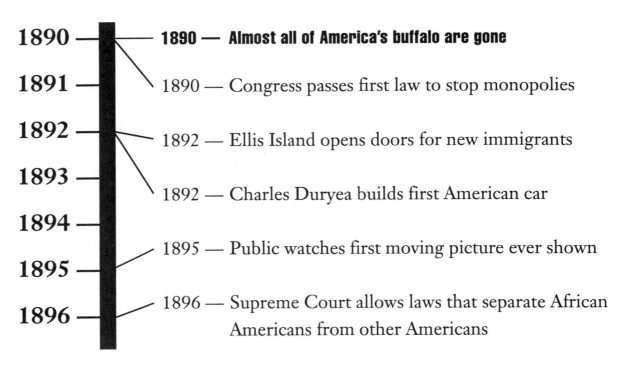

1890 — **1890 — Almost all of America's buffalo are gone**

1891 — 1890 — Congress passes first law to stop monopolies

1892 — 1892 — Ellis Island opens doors for new immigrants

1893 — 1892 — Charles Duryea builds first American car

1894 —

1895 — 1895 — Public watches first moving picture ever shown

1896 — 1896 — Supreme Court allows laws that separate African Americans from other Americans

What Else Was Happening?

Anyone who moved to the city for the first time in the 1890's was overwhelmed by the strange sights and sounds. There were bright lights, inside plumbing, paved streets and sidewalks, and trolley cars. Anyone used to shopping in small stores was surprised to find large "department stores" where people could buy so many different things in one place. And there were museums, libraries, and large theaters to marvel at as well. What a change from life on a farm or life in Eastern Europe.

There was a sad side to city life as well. Many people were poor. They worked long hours for little pay and lived crowded together in small apartments. Men, women, and even children worked, and still, sometimes, there was not enough food. Some workers joined labor unions in the hope of getting better working conditions and more pay.

#4

Land Where the Buffalo Roamed

The loud thundering noise jolted the young fur trader out of his deep sleep. He rubbed his eyes, sat upright, and stared into the prairie darkness. "What the—." He threw his blanket aside, and bolted behind a boulder. He glanced in one direction, then another. "I don't believe what I'm seeing."

No matter where he looked—in every direction—he saw the shadowy outlines of buffalo plodding across the flat, grassy land toward the distant river. Bunched together, they looked like giant, moving bushes. The fur trader crouched upright behind the rock. There had to be thousands of them! A dawn light was just beginning to streak across the prairie sky. He would stay right here and wait for them to pass.

Once the last straggling buffalo had gone by, the young man unpacked and opened his journal. He scrawled, "January, 1804," then

Courtesy, Library of Congress

Some weighing a ton, the Buffalo plodded over the land.

paused. No matter what he wrote, he would have trouble getting people to believe him. Finally, he scribbled: "Saw herds of buffalo. Took three days and three nights for all of them to pass."

Anyone who observed a buffalo herd on the move never forgot the sight of thousands of the shaggy-haired beasts—some weighing a ton, some six feet tall—rolling over the land. At times, the beasts moved almost as fast as galloping horses, trampling and grinding the ground and grass to dust. The Spanish explorers who came to America in the early 1500's told of seeing thousands and thousands of them in giant herds. Lewis and Clark, the explorers of the Louisiana Territory, reported that they darkened the whole plain for "as far as the eye could see."

Almost everyone seemed to have a story about buffalo. One settler described a herd eight miles wide and ten miles long. A traveler claimed he rode a train a hundred miles without losing sight of a buffalo. Another traveler counted the hours it took for a herd to pass him, and estimated he had seen millions of them go by. We do not know the exact number, but scientists agree that millions upon millions of buffalo roamed the plains in the early 1800's.

The early Indians stalked these animals on foot. Then, some years after the Spaniards introduced the modern horse to America, a whole new way of life began for the Indians who lived on the Plains. Mounted on horses, they could hunt and kill all the buffalo they wanted. Soon the buffalo became the main part of the Plains Indians way of life. Buffalo meat was dried and stored for the winter months. Hides were cut and sewn into coats, leggings, skirts, belts, and moccasins, or shaped into tepees or beds. Horns were carved and turned into cups, spoons, and ladles. Hoofs were mixed to make glue, and buffalo fat mixed into paint. Hides could be fashioned into saddles or bridles or bags, and bones could be shaped into toys for children. Rib bones became sled runners, and the shaggy hair from the buffalo's head was braided into rope.

The animal became the heart and soul of the Plain Indian's beliefs. Buffalo were in the stories they told, the songs they sang, the dances they danced, and the pictures they drew. The Indians killed only enough buffalo to feed themselves—no more. And so, the millions of buffalo that had roamed the plains for centuries still roamed the plains in large numbers through most of the 1800's.

In the late 1860's a great change began that would forever change life on the Plains: Railroad companies began building more railroad lines. To encourage more people to ride on them, the railroad companies printed advertisements for "Grand Buffalo Hunts." For a few dollars, Easterners could travel by train to "buffalo country." When the train came to a stop, passengers had the choice of getting off the train, or staying on board and shooting the buffalo right from the train windows! Since the buffalo was too large an animal to haul away, the hunter would shoot the animal, but leave the carcass to rot in the sun. Though buffalo hunting resembled shooting cows, the participants insisted that what they were doing was a sport. It was not, however, the sporting hunter who would change life on the Plains forever. After all, they were not killing off huge herds of buffalo.

Passengers had their choice of getting off the train or staying on board to shoot the buffalo.

In the 1870's and 1880's many more railroad lines were being built and cities in the East were growing larger. Buffalo robes and buffalo skins became very popular with the people living in these cities. To meet the demand, a new kind of buffalo hunter moved to buffalo country. He was more interested in making money than he was in killing the animal for the sport. He carried buffalo guns that weighed as much as 18 pounds and could drop a buffalo 300 yards away. Now, the real slaughter began. Hunters shot and skinned thousands and thousands of buffalo, and the newly built railroad lines could haul the buffalo skins—as well as buffalo meat—to the towns and cities in the East for a handsome profit. In a few years, with fewer buffalo to be found, the hunters were crossing into the lands set aside for the Indians and killing the buffalo there as well.

The slaughter went on and on until—where once millions of buffalo roamed the Plains—by 1890 there were less than 600 buffalo left in America! Fearful that the buffalo would disappear forever (become extinct), some Americans demanded that the U.S. government save the buffalo. Places called "reserves" were set up where buffalo were safe and could breed, and laws were passed that made it a crime to kill a buffalo. The laws came just in time. Soon, thousands of buffalo were being cared for in the zoos and reserves set aside for them. In time, the buffalo was saved—but not soon enough for the Indians. By now, the Indian way of life on the Plains was gone forever.

Americans once believed that America's wonderful natural resources—the fertile soil, the giant forests, the millions of animals, and the rich deposits of coal, iron, oil, and natural gas—would last forever. The story of the buffalo taught Americans a lesson they would never forget. This was especially true as cities grew and America's growing population began using up more and more of our natural resources.

Writing/Journal activities

1. TAKE IT OR LEAVE IT

Here are eight scenes an artist might have painted in the 1800's. Copy out the four scenes the artist might include in a painting about buffalo.

1. A herd of buffalo charging an Indian.

2. Four buffalo pulling a covered wagon.

3. People living in cities eating buffalo meat.

4. Indians skinning a buffalo.

5. Indians leaving hundreds of dead buffalo to rot in the sun.

6. Indians making moccasins from buffalo skins.

7. Indians wearing buffalo robes.

8. A herd of buffalo attacking a deer.

2. SEARCH AND FIND

Find the word (or words) closest to the meaning of the underlined word in each sentence. Then copy the sentence using that word (or words) in place of the underlined word.

1. The buffalo plodded along looking for food.
   moved along slowly   raced at full speed   sped along   drifted away

2. A few of the animals straggled.
   struggled   fell behind   ran ahead   grew hungry

3. The buffalo had shaggy hair.
   black and brown   bushy   short   shining

4. Indians stalked the buffalo.
   saved   hunted   ran from   respected

5. Buffalo would soon be extinct.
   forgotten   gone   worthless   valuable

6. The buffalo roamed the land.
   trampled   wandered over   ate off   ran over

3. ANSWER BACK

If you were an Indian, how would you answer someone who said this to you:

1. "Why is the buffalo so important to you?"

2. "Why does it bother you when buffalo hunters from the East come here to hunt for buffalo?"

Let's Talk — Discussion Activities

4. THINK IT THROUGH

Give as many answers as you can for each question.

— What might have happened if Americans living in cities and towns did not want any buffalo meat or buffalo robes?

— Since the Indians depended so much on the buffalo, should the hunters have stopped killing the buffalo? Why?

— Why should we be careful not to use up our natural resources today?

5. TAKE A SIDE

Here are two opinions on the same subject. Take one side or the other, and then give all the reasons you can for the side you take.

Today, animals that are in danger of being killed off until there are none left are called "endangered species." Sometimes, in order to protect an endangered species, businesses and workers are not allowed to carry on their work.

—"Everything should be done to keep an endangered species from being killed off even if it hurts some people."

—"Businesses and jobs are more important than saving an endangered species."

Cooperative Group Activities

6. IMAGINE

Imagine an Indian and a buffalo hunter are talking to each other. Have each side try to convince the other side that he or she is right.

7. A LOOK BACK

Select one of the events shown on the timeline for this story. Use other books or articles to gather more information about the event, and try to find out why the event was important. Present the information to the class or group.

1901

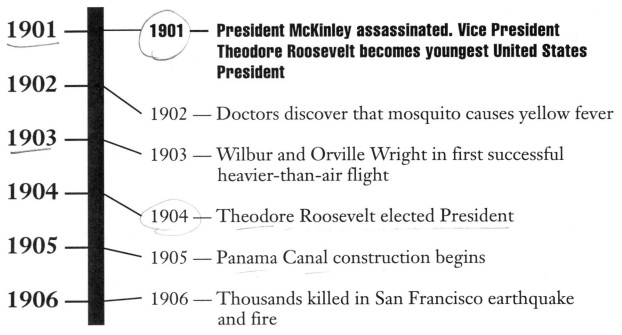

1901 — **1901** — **President McKinley assassinated. Vice President Theodore Roosevelt becomes youngest United States President**

1902 — 1902 — Doctors discover that mosquito causes yellow fever

1903 — 1903 — Wilbur and Orville Wright in first successful heavier-than-air flight

1904 — 1904 — Theodore Roosevelt elected President

1905 — 1905 — Panama Canal construction begins

1906 — 1906 — Thousands killed in San Francisco earthquake and fire

What Else Was Happening?

Cuba was once a part of the Spanish empire. In 1898 Cubans started a revolution. When the Spanish army stopped the revolution, some American newspapers described how cruel the Spanish army had been to the Cubans. Americans were upset with Spain when they read these stories, but President McKinley at first did not want to go to war with Spain over Cuba.

The American battleship Maine was anchored in a Cuban harbor when a giant explosion sent it to the bottom of the ocean with the loss of 260 sailors. Though there was no proof, American newspapers accused the Spanish government of blowing up the Maine and urged America to go to war. In April Congress declared war on Spain. Spain did not have a strong army or navy, and, in 100 days, Spain surrendered. As part of the peace agreement, Cuba was freed and the U.S. acquired the Philippines. America was becoming a world power; it would have to pay more attention to the events that were happening outside its borders.

#5

Teddy

Teddy was thin and frail as a boy.

Courtesy, The Houghton Library, Harvard University

Teddy never could remember exactly how the accident happened. One minute he and his friend, a young Army captain, stood toe to toe punching at one another. The next instant the captain's glove struck him squarely in the eye. Teddy felt a sharp, stinging pain. At first, he tried to shrug off the hurt, but when the pain would not go away, forty-three year old Teddy decided that was enough boxing exercise for one day.

A few days later, when the eye did not seem to be getting any better, Teddy saw an eye doctor. The doctor examined the eye carefully, then shook his head slowly. "I'm afraid I have some bad news," he began. He looked straight at Teddy.

"Mr. President, your left eye—it's lost its sight. You are blind in that eye."

The year was 1905. Theodore "Teddy" Roosevelt was beginning his second term as President of the United States. *Would he still be able to carry on as President? Wasn't there a chance that he would "fall apart," and not be able to go on with his duties?* Anyone who knew Theodore Roosevelt, who knew the kind of person he was, knew the answers...

Teddy Roosevelt was born in New York City in 1858. He was a weak and sickly child. One early morning, six year old Teddy awakened frightened and gasping desperately for breath. He sat up in his bed, sobbing. His body shook. Someone, or something—so it seemed—was strangling or suffocating him so that he could not breathe. Little Teddy Roosevelt was having another asthma attack. No one who has not had such an attack can imagine the pain, the fear, the suffering. His father and mother—both warm, caring parents—rushed to his side, but there was little they could do to help. No medicines had been discovered to stop or ease asthma attacks.

Teddy grew into a thin, frail boy. Like other asthma sufferers, he lived with the overwhelming fear of not knowing when the next attack would strike. By the time he was nine, Teddy was afraid to play with boys his own age. They were so much bigger and stronger, he thought. They would rough up someone as puny looking as he was. Teddy turned to reading books. He was bright, and he enjoyed reading almost anything, but especially books on nature and science.

One day Teddy's father decided to have a talk with him. Though he was a busy businessman, his father always made time to talk or play with Teddy and his brother and two sisters. He motioned for Teddy to sit down. "I'm proud of you for reading and building up your mind," he began, "but that is not enough. You also have to build up your body." If Teddy wanted to build up his body, he explained to his son, he would have to exercise. "It will be hard, dull work," he warned, "but I know you can do it."

Teddy's parents were wealthy, and so when Teddy agreed to exercise, his father had a gym built right in their home and filled it with exercise equipment. Teddy set about improving his body. He went from weight lifting to parallel bars, from punching bag to rings, from swinging ropes back to weight lifting. He also learned to wrestle and box, and to ride horses. He soon discovered that exercising was not dull at all. In fact, he enjoyed it a great deal!

Teddy grew from a frail, frightened child into a strong young man, sure of himself and what he wanted out of life. His love for exercise—what he called his "rigorous discipline"—never left him.

Teddy also kept right on reading. He read every kind of book he could get his hands on, and, what is more, seemed able to remember almost everything he read. By the time he graduated from Harvard in 1880 (with the highest honors), Teddy had developed his mind and his body well enough to feel confident about taking on any job.

He decided that what he wanted to do was to "try to help the cause of better government." Teddy served as a New York Assemblyman, as the president of the New York City Police Board, as a colonel in the Spanish American War, and as the Governor of New York. Finally, in 1901 when William McKinley was elected President of the United States, Teddy was elected Vice President. When McKinley was assassinated, Teddy became the President.

Teddy's strong sense of confidence stayed with him. He never stopped believing in himself—no matter what happened.

When he was in his twenties, both his mother and young wife died on the same day, leaving him with a baby daughter. He knew he had to carry on with his life's work. He refused to mope or give up.

Once, while horseback riding, Teddy was thrown from his horse and the horse landed on his arm. Teddy defiantly got back on the horse, jumped twenty fences while his broken arm dangled at his side, before having the arm taken care of.

Another time, someone tried to shoot him. The bullet smashed into his chest. Fortunately, the bullet was slowed down by an eyeglass case and a long speech Teddy had folded up and tucked into his coat. With blood trickling from his chest, Teddy laughed off any suggestions that he cancel his speech and disappoint the people who came to hear him. Teddy stood on the podium, delivered the speech in his usual fiery manner, pounding on the podium, and gesturing with his hands or pointing an accusing finger.

And so, when this new tragedy struck, Teddy never doubted for a moment what to do. He said nothing about the eye accident to the American people, and went right on as if nothing had a happened. Theodore "Teddy" Roosevelt served out almost all of his second term as President of the United States blind in one eye. He had learned long before not to let any obstacle stand in his way.

Probably no president was more loved and admired than Theodore Roosevelt. He was a man of action who seemed to bubble with ideas. His accomplishments included saving many of our rivers, parks, and forests; building up the U.S. Navy; starting the construction of the Panama Canal; and stopping some large companies from becoming monopolies. He also received the Nobel Peace Prize for helping to stop the Japanese-Russian war. Busy as he was as President, Theodore Roosevelt somehow managed to keep up with his reading. It was not unusual for him to read one or two books an evening. He also kept writing books, and writing thousands of letters. During all of this, the President somehow found the time to play with his five young children.

Not bad for someone who started out as an uncertain, frightened, sickly boy.

He never stopped believing in himself—no matter what happened.

Courtesy, The Houghton Library, Harvard University

Writing/Journal Activities

1. TAKE IT OR LEAVE IT

Here are eight words that describe Teddy Roosevelt as a child or adult. Copy out the four words that describe him best as an adult.

1. brave	2. daring	3. sickly	4. active
5. timid	6. shy	7. bashful	8. outgoing

2. SEARCH AND FIND

Find the word (or words) closest to the meaning of the underlined word in each sentence. Then copy the sentence using that word (or words) in place of the underlined word.

1. Teddy Roosevelt suffered from asthma when he was young.
   a breathing illness   a skin disease   an eye disease   an ear infection

2. Teddy was a frail young boy.
   weak   careless   strong   smart

3. He refused to mope when he faced a difficult time.
   sulk   yell   cry   blame someone else

4. He was defiant after he fell off his horse.
   careless   bold   thoughtless   careful

5. Teddy pounded the podium in his usual manner.
   chair   stool   counter   speaking platform

6. He often gestured with his hands.
   made motions   pointed up   clapped   gripped something

3 ANSWER BACK

If you were Teddy Roosevelt, how would you answer a someone who said—

1. "You are weak and shy—you will never amount to anything."

2. "You spend too much time reading books."

3. "What are your three most important accomplishments?"

Let's Talk—Discussion Activities

4. THINK IT THROUGH

Give as many answers as you can for each question.

—Why do you think Roosevelt was such a popular president?

—What qualities did Teddy Roosevelt have that you like or admire?

—Does exercising your body really build up your confidence? Explain.

5. TAKE A SIDE

Here are two opinions on the same subject. Take one side or the other, and then give all the reasons you can for the side you take.

—"It is more important to exercise your mind than your body."

—"It is more important to exercise your body."

Cooperative Group Activities

6. IMAGINE

Imagine that you are President Theodore Roosevelt. A newspaper reporter asks you what advice on how to be successful you would give to a young boy or girl.

Imagine you are voting for a U.S. President. Pick the four most important qualities you think a U.S. President should have. There are no "right" or "wrong" answers, but be able to justify or explain your answers.

intelligent	inspiring	reasonable	healthy
experienced	logical	caring	energetic

7. A LOOK BACK

Select one of the events shown on the timeline for this story. Use other books or articles to gather more information about the event, and try to find out why the event was important. Present the information to the class or group.

1911

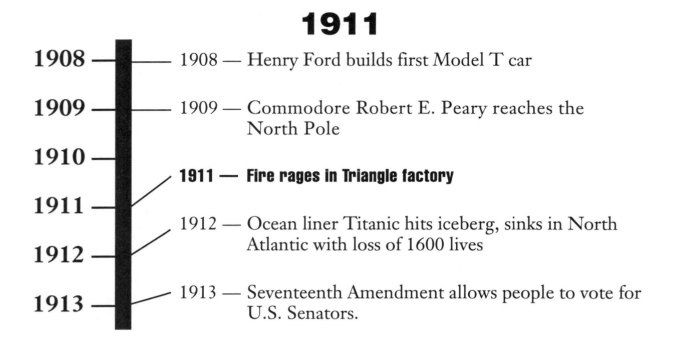

1908 — Henry Ford builds first Model T car

1909 — Commodore Robert E. Peary reaches the North Pole

1911 — Fire rages in Triangle factory

1912 — Ocean liner Titanic hits iceberg, sinks in North Atlantic with loss of 1600 lives

1913 — Seventeenth Amendment allows people to vote for U.S. Senators.

What Else Was Happening?

America was becoming a great industrial nation for many reasons. Its land was rich in natural resources. American inventors were encouraged to create new products. Investors were willing to invest, or risk, large sums of money in new industries. America also had a large supply of workers, or laborers, willing to work hard. As a result, new industries produced many wonderful new products for Americans to use.

These industries also created some problems. People who pointed out these problems and wanted to make changes were called "reformers." Reformers fought for better and safer working conditions as well as shorter working days for workers. Other reformers worked to improve the living conditions of poor people who lived crowded together in the cities. Reformers also tried to remove dishonest government officials from office. Some reformers worked to have food and drug laws passed to protect people's health.

#6

The Triangle Fire

The men and women bustling along the New York sidewalk this brisk afternoon in March were not alarmed by the first wisps of smoke coming from the eighth floor windows. *Isn't that the Triangle Company building where they manufacture women's blouses? Well, then, the smoke must be coming from one of their machines.*

A moment later, one of the men on the sidewalk spotted flames at a window. "It's a fire," he shouted, "A fire!"

Still, no reason to be too alarmed. *There aren't any workers there—it's Saturday afternoon.* Then, what looked like two bundles of cloth tumbled out of one of the windows. *Must be a watchman trying to save some cloth from the fire.*

Moments later—with distant fire engine sirens screaming in the background—the spectators on the sidewalk below caught the full horror of what was really happening. The falling "bundles of cloth" were not bundles of cloth at all. They were young girls leaping from the building to escape the fire...

On Saturday, March 25, 1911, some 600 workers—almost all of them young girls—sat hunched over their sewing machines on the eighth floor of the Triangle building. The girls sat close to each other in six long rows, sewing together bits and pieces of different cloth, and turning them into women's blouses. They chatted in broken English, or in the languages they and their parents had spoken before they arrived in America. These girls were part of a giant wave of immigrant families who had come to America in search of a better life. They came from the countries in Eastern Europe—mainly Russia and Poland. Some also came from Italy.

Shortly after 4:30, one of the girls spotted a fire in a bin used for keeping rags. A careless workman had dropped a match or a lighted cigarette in the bin. The material had smoldered for a time, then burst into flames.

"Fire!" the girl shouted. Two girls grabbed water buckets and threw the water into the bin. The material sizzled and smoked, but by now the fire had crept to the bits of cloth that were scattered all about the floor. Two workmen rushed to the fire hose hooked in place on a wall. They tugged at the hose and aimed it at the fire. One of the men tried turning the rusty valve, but it would not budge. At the same time, the hose—rotted with age—was crumbling in their hands.

Fed by the materials used to make the blouses—lace, silk, linen, and cotton—that were everywhere, the fire quickly licked across the eighth floor. It caught the finished blouses strung overhead in long lines, then leaped through the windows to the ninth floor. Meantime, the workers screamed in terror as they struggled to find a way out.

The only fire escape was an old and rickety iron one, barely a foot and a half wide. It would have taken hours for all the girls to leave using such a narrow exit. A few girls managed to escape using it before the fire turned it into a twisted mass of useless iron.

There was another way out. A narrow passageway led to the two small freight elevators in the building. Each elevator could carry no more than a dozen people, but on this day only one of them was working. The elevator made two trips, then stopped working. When it failed to return to the eighth floor, the workers forced open the doors, then rushed headlong into the elevator shaft. A few managed to cling to the pulleys and slid down to safety. The others fell screaming to their deaths.

Most of the workers rushed towards one of the stairways only to discover that a closed door blocked their exit. The girls banged and pounded on the door until their hands turned bloody. It would not budge. The door had been locked and bolted shut. The owners had wanted to check the purses of the girls as they left the building each evening to keep them from stealing. They had locked this stairway to make the check easier for them.

The girls who chose the second stairway

Courtesy, The Bettmann Archive

The firemen worked as hard as they could, but everything seemed to be going wrong.

did not do any better. They rushed headlong down the narrow stairs only to find two side by side doors that opened *inward*. To get out, they would have to swing the doors backward. A few girls grabbed the door handles and tried to pull back. They might as well have tried moving a giant tidal wave. The mob of girls behind them crushed and pinned them against the door.

Meantime the firemen outside worked as hard as they could, but everything seemed to be going wrong. Their ladders reached only as far as the seventh floor. But the worst was yet to come.

With the fire closing in on them, many of the girls climbed onto window sills where they screamed out their terror—and jumped. The firemen moved nets into place, and tried to catch them. It was no use; the nets were not strong enough to stop anything coming down from eight or nine floors.

One hundred forty-one workers died that March afternoon in 1911. Almost all of them were young girls between 15 and 25 years of age. The tragedy struck the heart of the nation. Everyone seemed to be asking the same questions: Why wasn't more care taken to protect the workers? Why were there so few exits? Why did the doors open inward? Why wasn't there better fire fighting equipment in the factory? Why didn't the firemen have better fire fighting and rescue equipment? These immigrants had come to America for a better life. Now their hopes were gone forever.

Americans did not want such a terrible tragedy to happen again. Laws were passed in New York and in other cities and states that made working conditions in factories better and safer for working men and women. In time, the tragic Triangle fire encouraged people to find ways to make American factories safer for future generations.

Writing/Journal Activities

1. WHAT'S THE BIG IDEA?

Copy out the story's most important message or main idea.

A. Better ways were needed to prevent and fight fires in factories.

B. Better ways were needed to train fire-fighters.

C. People had to learn to avoid taking elevators in a fire.

D. Better fire escapes had to be built.

2. GET THE PICTURE

Here are eight scenes that an artist might have painted. Copy out the four scenes that best describe what happened in the Triangle fire.

1. a house on fire
2. a rotted fire hose
3. a twisted fire escape
4. blouses on fire
5. fire sprinklers in ceiling
6. a fire extinquisher
7. doors locked and bolted
8. lightning in the sky

3. WHO SAID THAT?

Here are six statements. Copy the three statements that a Triangle fire survivor might have made.

1. "We have the day off on Saturdays."
2. "We need better fire escapes."
3. "Do not lock the factory doors."
4. "Do something to keep this from happening again."
5. "I'm glad I worked for the Triangle blouse factory."
6. "The factory owners were very thoughtful of us."

Let's Talk—Discussion Activities

4. THINK IT THROUGH

Give as many answers as you can for each question.

— Explain this: The Triangle fire was a terrible tragedy, but some good things happened because of the fire.

— Who was guilty of the fire—the careless workman? the factory owners? the working girls? the city government? the fire inspectors?

5. TAKE A SIDE

Here are two opinions on the same subject. Take one side or the other, and then give all the reasons you can for the side you take.

— "Some fire prevention devices are too expensive to use."

— "No matter what it costs, we should have every fire prevention device."

6. THEN AND NOW

— What important fire laws and devices do we have today that people did not have in 1911?

— In what other ways are factories safer today than they were in the days of this story?

Cooperative Group Activities

7. IMAGINE

Imagine that you were a newspaper reporter describing the Triangle fire. What three important things would you want to tell your readers?

8. A LOOK BACK

Select one of the events shown on the timeline for this story. Use other books or articles to gather more information about the event, and try to find out why the event was important. Present the information to the class or group.

1915

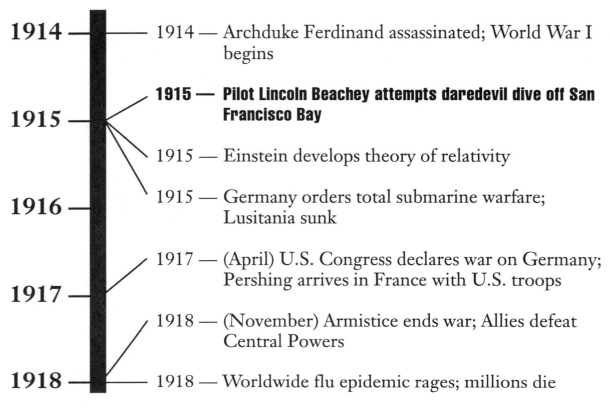

1914 — Archduke Ferdinand assassinated; World War I begins

1915 — Pilot Lincoln Beachey attempts daredevil dive off San Francisco Bay

1915 — Einstein develops theory of relativity

1915 — Germany orders total submarine warfare; Lusitania sunk

1917 — (April) U.S. Congress declares war on Germany; Pershing arrives in France with U.S. troops

1918 — (November) Armistice ends war; Allies defeat Central Powers

1918 — Worldwide flu epidemic rages; millions die

What Else Was Happening?

When World War I began in Europe in 1914, most Americans did not want the U.S. to get into the war. They wanted to stay neutral, that is, not to take sides. However, as the terrible war dragged on, Americans became more and more sympathetic to the Allies (England, France, Russia, and many smaller countries) against the Central Powers (Germany and Austria-Hungary). By 1917, the U.S. decided to enter the war on the side of the Allies. A million Americans troops were sent overseas to fight in France. There had never been a war where so many men were killed and wounded. Tanks, poison gas, machine guns and airplanes were used for the first time. American troops and war supplies tipped the balance in favor of the Allies, and an armistice was signed on November 11, 1918. Americans were proud that they had helped to win the war, but now wanted to steer clear of any more European problems.

#7

Master Of The Sky

A crowd of fifty thousand spectators had gathered all along the San Francisco Bay to watch the air show this crisp, sunny afternoon in March, 1915. As the people searched the blue skies, someone in the crowd pointed skyward. *There! There it is!* The speck in the distance grew larger and larger. Soon everyone could make out the flimsy, single engine airplane.

As the plane dropped lower and circled over the crowd, the spectators broke into loud cheering. A moment later, the plane began a slow steady climb. As the plane rose, the spectators grew silent until the only sound in the world seemed to be coming from the plane's 80 horsepower engine. The plane leveled off, and then—*did you see that?* He did a complete backward loop. The crowd roared its approval. Again, the plane went higher. Much higher. And again, the crowd grew silent. The plane leveled off, dropped its nose, and dove straight down. Closer, closer it came. Every man and woman in the crowd seemed to be holding their breaths. *He'll pull out,* they thought. *Lincoln Beachey always does...*

Lincoln Beachey was 16 years old when the Wright brothers made their first airplane flight at Kitty Hawk, North Carolina, in 1903. Over the next few years, Beachey and a few other brave souls took to flying when planes were wood and wire and canvas, and the pilot sat in a small wide open seat in front of a ten horsepower engine. Beachey crashed the first plane he ever tried to fly, but somehow, managed to walk away. Not knowing any better, he took a second plane up, and crashed that one as well. Most people would have decided that it was time to quit, but not Beachey. He kept at it day after day until he gained a "sense" and "feel" for how far he could push his plane— and still live to tell about it.

During these early years of flying, pilots called "barnstormers" hopped from one town or city to another performing their daring air tricks over large, open fields. Most people in the early 1900's had never even seen an airplane, so the sight of one pulling out of a dive or skimming breathlessly close to the ground at 80 miles an hour was a sight indeed. There was good money to be made, and Lincoln Beachey joined a group of these barnstorming pilots in 1911. By the end of the year, Lincoln Beachey's daring feats made him the favorite of every audience. All the other pilots who, like Beachey, challenged the skies in these uncertain planes, admitted that Beachey was the best. In fact, they called him "Master of the Sky." Beachey had earned the title.

Six months after his first try at flying, Beachey announced to his fellow barnstorming pilots: "I'm going to fly over Niagara Falls and under the International Bridge." The other flyers thought he was crazy, but on a June afternoon, in 1911, Beachey began his flight over the Falls. Halfway over, he was startled by the unfamiliar sound of his tiny engine spitting and sputtering. The misty air that hung over the Falls was clogging the gasoline engine! The plane was losing power! Beachey had not planned on this. He thought quickly. Somehow, he managed to make all the right maneuvers, and coaxed the plane over the Falls and under the bridge. But even Beachey knew enough never to try the stunt again. For that matter, no one else ever tried it either.

The narrow escape did not cut down on Beachey's imaginative approach to flying. A few weeks later, he had another idea. He told a half-dozen other flyers: "We'll all get in our planes and climb to five or six thousand feet. Then we'll all shut our engines off at the same time." The pilots looked at each other to make sure that they heard him correctly. "And then—" Beachey laughed, "we will keep right on diving, and the one who pulls out at the lowest altitude will be the winner."

Beachey was serious, but he had no takers that day. It did not matter; Lincoln Beachey discovered plenty of other exciting stunts to do—stunts that drew cheers and applause from audiences everywhere. He dove, he spiraled, he took imaginary "rides" over imaginary roller coasters in the sky. Or he—

— flew just above the road touching the tops of automobiles with his landing wheels.
— pitched a baseball from a moving plane to a catcher on the ground.
— stood up in his plane spread out like an eagle while flying 100 feet above the ground.
— flew into a huge building and soared around inside (no one had done it before or since).
— touched the smokestack of a moving train with his landing wheels.

In late August of 1911, Beachey decided on a unique way to set the record for how high a plane could fly. First, he filled his gas tank to the brim, then climbed until he ran out of gas. Once out of gas, he spiraled down to a nice landing and a new altitude record of 11, 642 feet, or a little over two miles. Probably his most famous stunt however, was the "climb and dive." He climbed a mile above his audience, dove straight down, leveled off the last few seconds, and then—still at full throttle—maneuvered the plane so that one of the wing tips caught a handkerchief placed a few feet above the ground.

Surprising as it sounds, Beachey did not know a lot about the science of flying. There were no instruments, no gauges, to warn him of danger. Instead, because he flew in the open without a cockpit, he learned to depend on a "sense" that told him what his plane could do and what it could not do. This "feeling" kept him alive. Unfortunately, other Barnstormers tried imitating Beachey's feats of daring even though they did not have this same feel or sense for what these primitive airplanes could do. The results were disastrous.

Early in 1913, after only two years of flying, Beachey announced that he was through. "I'm quitting," he said. "I think that I have been pretty lucky, but I am tired of taking chances." Some people thought that he was not serious and just trying to get more publicity, but a few months later he spoke at a gathering in San Francisco. He read off the names of 24 pilots, then looked up at his audience. "These men were like brothers to me," he began. "And all of them were killed trying to imitate me." It was too large a burden for even the great Beachey to bear.

Beachey turned to vaudeville where he spoke to audiences as they watched movies of his daring feats. He claimed his retirement was permanent, but he really missed flying. Then, near the end of 1913, a pilot in France did a "forward loop," that is he somersaulted a plane for the first time in history. Beachey fumed when he heard the news. He had al-

Lincoln Beachey took to flying when planes were wood and wire and canvas, and the pilot sat in a small wide open seat in front of a ten horsepower engine.

ways planned to do such a trick, and now, someone had beaten him to it!

Beachey came roaring out of retirement. After he perfected a more difficult backward loop-the-loop, he added a spinning dive to his bag of tricks. Finally he came up with what he called the "Race of the Century." As Barney Oldfield, America's greatest racing driver, sped along a two mile track, Beachey flew a few feet over his head. With engines racing at full throttle, the two of them raced madly towards the same finish line.

In March, 1915, Lincoln Beachey was invited to appear at the Panama Pacific Exposition in San Francisco to celebrate the opening of the Panama Canal. Here fifty thousand spectators watched as Beachey climbed to 3500 feet, dove, then leveled his plane to fly upside down. The plane dove again. Closer and closer it came. *He'll pull out. He always does.*

What's that?

The left wing, then the right, were tearing away from the fuselage. Now, the wings were floating aimlessly towards the waters of the Bay...

Beachey must have known that he was gambling his life every time he took up his flimsy plane. After all, by 1915. the airplane was barely 12 years old—hardly old enough to be too trustworthy. Nevertheless, Beachey was willing to take the gamble. After all, he had won hundreds of times before—but March 13, 1915 was different. The plane—what was left of it—slammed into the bay, and the chill waters swirled over the wreckage. Lincoln Beachey—the man Wilbur Wright had called America's greatest pilot—was gone. The "Master of the Sky" had made his last death-defying dive. Beachey would have to leave it to future pilots—perhaps less daring, less skillful—but with more powerful engines, stronger materials, and better designed planes to conquer the skies.

Two years after Beachey's death, other daring American pilots were sharpening their skills and testing their planes in the skies over Europe. No longer was the airplane a wonderful invention for entertaining crowds. By 1917, men had learned how to make the airplane yet another weapon of war.

Writing/Journal

1. WHAT'S THE BIG IDEA?

Copy out this story's most important message or main idea.

A. A person should be willing to take chances all the time.

B. A person should try to know his or her limits.

C. A person should be willing to do things to entertain others.

D. A person should not be afraid.

2. GET THE PICTURE

Here are eight scenes an artist might have painted. Copy out the four scenes that best describe Lincoln Beachey's life.

1. cheering crowds
2. a plane made of aluminum
3. a plane doing a loop
4. a blimp
5. the San Francisco Bay
6. a jet engine
7. a plane racing a car
8. a plane racing a person

3. WHO SAID THAT?

Here are six statements. Copy the three statements that Lincoln Beachey might have made.

1. "I'm afraid to take chances."

2. "I'm quitting because the other pilots are trying to imitate me."

3. "I depend on many instruments when I fly."

4. "I like to entertain crowds with my tricks."

5. "I like these all metal planes."

6. "I tried to quit but I could not."

Let's Talk—Discussion Questions

4. THINK IT THROUGH

Give as many answers as you can for each question.

— Why do "daredevils" do dangerous tricks even though they know they are risking their lives?

— How did "daredevils" like Beachey help the airplane industry?

5. TAKE A SIDE

Here are two opinions on the same subject. Take one side or the other, and then give all the reasons you can for the side you take.

— "The government should not allow daredevils to risk their lives."

— "If someone wants to do something dangerous, it should be up to him or her."

6. THEN AND NOW

— In what ways is today's flying different from in Beachey's day? In what ways is flying the same?

— What are some dangerous feats that people do today?

— Are today's astronauts doing things as dangerous as the things Beachey did?

— What is the big difference between a pilot today, and an early pilot like Beachey?

Cooperative Group Activities

7. IMAGINE

Imagine that you are Beachey. A young boy or girl writes you a letter telling you that he or she wants to be a pilot just like you. Write a letter back to the boy or girl in which you encourage or discourage the young person.

8. A LOOK BACK

Select one of the events shown on the timeline for this story. Use other books or articles to gather more information about the event, and try to find out why the event was important. Present the information to the class or group.

1920

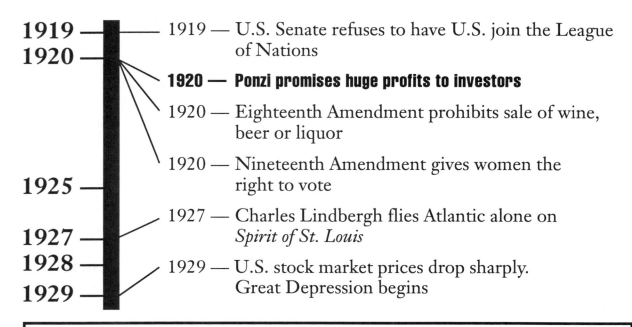

1919 — U.S. Senate refuses to have U.S. join the League of Nations

1920 — Ponzi promises huge profits to investors

1920 — Eighteenth Amendment prohibits sale of wine, beer or liquor

1920 — Nineteenth Amendment gives women the right to vote

1927 — Charles Lindbergh flies Atlantic alone on *Spirit of St. Louis*

1929 — U.S. stock market prices drop sharply. Great Depression begins

1919
1920
1925
1927
1928
1929

What Else Was Happening?

After World War I, many countries joined an organization called the "League of Nations." The goal of the League was to have countries solve their problems by discussing them instead of going to war over them. President Woodrow Wilson wanted the U.S. to join the League, but most Americans did not want to get involved in Europe's problems again. That is, they wanted to "isolate" themselves, and so the U.S. Senate voted not to join the League.

The years after World War I are known as the "Roaring Twenties." Millions of people were working, and they could buy things they could never afford before. Americans believed that these good times would go on forever. They were in for a terrible shock—the good times came to an end in 1929 when millions of people lost their jobs.

Because Americans could not buy wine, beer, or whiskey legally in the 1920's, some Americans purchased what was called "bootleg" liquor. This created many problems because the sale of this illegal liquor was often controlled by criminals.

#8
Confidence for Sale

The old man's movements were slow and painful as he tried to find a comfortable position on his hospital bed. His breathing was slow. When he looked about, his fading eyesight gave him a clouded picture of a large, dirty hospital ward. Before this January day in 1949 ended, the world would hear that John Ponzi, the one time millionaire, had died a penniless, broken man in a charity hospital in South America. How different this was from the dapper young Ponzi millions of Americans read about in their newspapers in the 1920's...

Each morning the short, jaunty figure would order the chauffeur to stop the limousine in front of his Boston office. No one could miss noticing him as he stepped out of the limo. He wore a well tailored suit and a glittering diamond tie-clasp. As he strolled alongside the line of people waiting outside his office, he offered a smile here, a kind word there. The people standing in the long line beamed back and gave him warm greetings of their own. As if his glistening ring, his gold-handled cane, and gold cigarette holder were not enough, Ponzi would place a very large check—plainly visible—in his upper right-hand coat pocket.

As Ponzi walked towards his office, he had much more in mind than merely showing off. He wanted to create the impression that he was rich so that people would have confidence in him. In fact, everything Ponzi did was part of a plan to make people believe that he was wealthy—and quite willing to let others get rich too.

Ponzi came to America at the age of 21. Like many other poor immigrants, he was willing to do any kind of work no matter how little it paid. He worked as a dishwasher, a waiter, a clerk. When one job closed, he moved on until he found another even if it meant traveling from one city to another. Ponzi was living this simple kind of life early in 1920 when he hit upon an idea that would turn his world around forever. He ran a small advertisement in a newspaper that went like this: *If you give me $100 and leave it with me for a month and a half, you will receive the hundred dollars back as well as a $50 profit. If you leave the $100 with me for three months, I promise to give you another $100.* No bank in the world paid interest like this!

A handful of people took Ponzi up on his first offer and gave him a total of $900. True to his word, Ponzi paid off each investor at

Courtesy, Boston Public Library

Ponzi offered a smile here, a kind word there. Each month the number of people investing in his scheme grew.

like this! Why, it was like finding money on the street! Through the early months of 1920, word spread about Ponzi's exciting offer. By June the lines in front of Ponzi's office grew until they snaked back for blocks. "Here," people told him, "Please take my money."

On some days money came in faster than Ponzi and his helpers could count it. After every desk drawer and waste basket was filled, Ponzi piled the money in closets until the piles reached the ceiling. By early June, some 8,000 people had invested millions of dollars on the word of a man none of them really knew. How could Ponzi pay back so much money? At first Ponzi explained that he did it by buying coupons for postage stamps in one country and then using the coupons to buy postage stamps worth more money in another country. When experts explained that Ponzi could not possibly make money this way, some investors rushed to Ponzi's office and demanded that he return their money. Ponzi only laughed. He returned money to anyone who asked, and—with a twinkle in his eye—admitted his postage stamp story was just a made up story to throw people off the track. His real scheme, he explained, was solid as a rock. When people saw how quickly he returned their money, most of them begged him to take their money back.

the spectacular rate of interest he had advertised. It did not take long for these investors to spread the word of their good fortune to friends and relatives. Soon, more and more investors were coming to Ponzi's office to plunk down money. Each time, Ponzi rewarded their confidence in him with the promised money and interest. Investors were overjoyed. *No bank in the world paid interest*

Each month the number of people investing in Ponzi's scheme grew. By late in July over 30,000 people had given Ponzi more than 9 1/2 million dollars. Remember, Ponzi's scheme depended on one single ingredient: confidence. On August 11, 1920, The Boston Post published a story that claimed Ponzi had started a similar investment scheme in Montreal, Canada, years before, and that Ponzi had been arrested for forgery and had served 20 months in a Canadian jail. The man who seemed so confident, so the Boston newspaper claimed, was a former convict.

The news was electrifying. The thousands of people who had placed fortunes into the hands of an ex-convict on faith alone now demanded their money back. Too late, they learned what should have been obvious: Ponzi was able to pay off the investors each month because more and more people insisted on giving him money. He was paying off the early investors with money that came in from later investors. Sooner or later the bubble would burst. The Post story served as the pin that burst the bubble.

Ponzi proclaimed his innocence in one breath and the soundness of his plan in another. But his world shattered under charges that he was a criminal. Ponzi had taken in 15 million dollars. The people who still had money with Ponzi got back only 8 cents for every dollar they had given to him.

Ponzi served 3 1/2 years in jail for using the mails to defraud, and another seven years in Massachusetts for stealing money. Out of jail he never made much money again. In 1939 he moved to Brazil where he managed to make a few dollars by giving English lessons. When he became ill, he was placed in a hospital set aside for poor people. Here the once wealthy millionaire died, penniless and all but forgotten.

Businesses helped build America into a great industrial nation. These businesses depended on people willing to invest money in them. Most of the men and women who ran these businesses were honest so that investors received their money back with interest. However, to this day, when someone wants to describe a fraud for making money by borrowing from one person to pay off another, the trick is called a "Ponzi scheme."

Writing/Journal Activities

1. WHAT'S THE BIG IDEA?

Copy out this story's most important message or main idea.

— Trust the person who shows confidence.

— Be careful of someone who promises way too much.

— An investment is safe if there are a lot of investors.

— Ponzi was an honest man.

2. GET THE PICTURE

Here are eight words used to describe someone. Copy out the four that describe Ponzi the best.

1. showy	2. ethical	3. confident	4. flashy
5. modest	6. plain	7. trustworthy	8. crooked

3. WHO SAID THAT?

Here are six statements. Copy the three statements that a person who gave money to Ponzi might have made.

1. "I trusted him because he looked so confident."

2. "I thought it was safe after the first investors made so much money."

3. "I invested after watching Ponzi on television."

4. "My bank offered more interest than Ponzi did."

5. "He paid off with counterfeit money."

6. "I got eight cents back for every dollar I gave him."

Let's Talk—Discussion Activities

4. THINK IT THROUGH

Give as many answers as you can for each question.

— Explain this: It is easier to cheat someone who is greedy.

— Explain this: Freedom of the press sometimes prevents people from getting fooled.

— What should you do to keep from being fooled by a Ponzi scheme?

— Explain this: If it sounds "too good to be true," it almost always is not true.

5. TAKE A SIDE

Here are two opinions on the same subject. Take one side or the other, and then give all the reasons you can for the side you take.

— "Laws and the government should protect a person from dishonest persons."

— "You should be on guard against dishonest people, and not expect the government to do it for you."

Cooperative Group Activities

6. IMAGINE

Imagine that you were deciding whether or not to invest your money with Ponzi. What clues should tell you that something is wrong—even before the newspaper stories.

7. A LOOK BACK

Select one of the events shown on the timeline for this story. Use other books or articles to gather more information about the event, and try to find out why the event was important. Present the information to the class or group.

1933

1932	1932 — U.S. in Great Depression—many factories and banks close, 13 million Americans out of work
1933	1933 — U.S. builds its first aircraft carrier
	1933 — Franklin D. Roosevelt takes office as U.S. President
1934	1933 — Twenty-First Amendment makes it legal to sell beer, wine, whiskey again
1935	1936 — Franklin D. Roosevelt in landslide win over Alf Landon for President
1936	1937 — German dirigible (airship) Hindenburg explodes at Lakehurst, New Jersey, ending all dirigible passenger travel
1937	1937 — Amelia Earhart's plane vanishes over Pacific

What Else Was Happening?

The 1930's were a very difficult time for Americans. Factories that had manufactured so many goods in the 1920's closed down, and the men and women working there lost their jobs. Few people had money to buy things so that more and more people were put out of work. Men and women begged in the streets. President Franklin D. Roosevelt was elected President in 1932. He had some ideas for stopping the Depression. Congress passed laws hoping to create more jobs, and the government created some jobs. However, bad conditions continued throughout the thirties.

The Depression was taking place in other countries as well. Some of these countries turned to dictators, giving up their freedoms in the hope of making things better. Benito Mussolini became dictator of Italy. Hitler seized power and became dictator of Germany. The Soviet Union had already turned to communism and was ruled by a dictator, Joseph Stalin. Japan was ruled by military leaders. The American people however, despite terrible economic times, kept their faith in democracy.

#9

The Girl Who Was Afraid

Three year old Eleanor peered through the fog below. Her tiny hands gripped the ship's railing as tightly as she could. Eight feet below, her father stood on a life boat, hands outstretched, yelling for her to jump into his arms. Eleanor and her parents were on their way to Europe when another ship steaming through the fog-covered New York Harbor rammed the ship they were on. The passengers were told to leave the ship, and now poor Eleanor stood on the deck—staring at the water below—too frightened to move. A sailor on the deck behind Eleanor saw what was happening. He rushed over, uncurled her tiny fingers from the rail, lifted the girl in his arms, and then gently dropped her over the side. The flailing, screaming Eleanor fell safely into her father's arms.

Once back on shore, Eleanor's mother and father tried to calm her. They reassured the little girl that everyone had left the boat safely and that no one had been hurt. It did not matter. Eleanor would not stop crying. She could not get over the nightmare of staring through the fog at the choppy water below, and she kept imagining the murky green water swallowing her up. Eleanor's fear of water stayed on for many years. In fact, Eleanor lived in a world filled with fear and anxiety. Her mother, a rich and pretty society woman, made it clear to Eleanor that she was not a pretty child. She called little Eleanor "Granny" because, so her mother said, she looked so much like a funny, old "granny" or grandmother. One of Eleanor's aunts said she was the family's "ugly duckling." Eleanor felt hurt and embarrassed. Whenever Eleanor met someone, the first thing that went through her mind was, "That person must think I'm ugly." Eleanor grew up afraid of any one she met—even children her own age.

Each year brought new fears. Horses, dogs, cats, people, the dark, water—everything seemed to frighten poor Eleanor. Timid, fearful, Eleanor believed she could only disappoint and displease her parents. No matter what she did or said, she felt that she was a disgrace to her beautiful mother.

Eleanor's wealthy parents traveled quite a bit, and little Eleanor often stayed with an older aunt. "Poor child," her aunt once said. "What will ever become of our poor Eleanor?" Each year brought new fears, and all the more reason to wonder—*what would become of poor Eleanor?*

When Eleanor was six, her mother came down with diphtheria and died. We hear little about diphtheria today, but it was once a terrible disease that attacked the throat and made it difficult for someone to breathe. Eleanor was very sad, but she felt thankful she still had

"What will ever become of our poor Eleanor?" (Eleanor, far right, with her father and two brothers.)

her father. She loved him more than anyone in the world, and called him "the center of the world." He was a warm and handsome man who showered her with affection. However, he was an alcoholic, and spent much of his time in and out of places that try to cure people who can not stop drinking.

Because of her father's drinking problem, Eleanor went to live with her grandmother. The brightest parts of her life were the days her father came to visit. She would tell everyone that he was her hero. Then, when Eleanor was ten, her father died. She was crushed. Her mother was gone, and now, her only hero in all the world was gone too. To make matters worse, one of her two younger brothers had also died of diphtheria.

Eleanor grew into a timid, lonely, frightened teenager. She grew tall, but stayed thin and unattractive. When there was a dance, or any kind of get-together, she remained very unsure of herself. Eleanor's aunt kept asking anyone who would listen, "What's to become of our poor Eleanor?"

Then, while still a teenager, Eleanor made an amazing discovery. She realized that the best way to conquer her fears was to face them and not run away from them. "I must do what I can not do," was the way she put it. Her mind made up, she set about meeting each of her fears.

To conquer her fear of the dark, she purposely went into dark places. To conquer her fear of dogs, she went out of her way to pet them. To conquer her tremendous fear of sick people, she visited hospitals. She attacked each of her fears the same way—whether it was fear of water, fear of crowds, or fear of animals. She met them head on.

So what ever became of "poor Eleanor"?

For one thing, when she was eighteen years old, Eleanor said yes to a young man named Franklin when he asked her to marry him. Years later, in 1928, Franklin Roosevelt became governor of New York state. However, Eleanor became much more than a governor's wife. She joined women's groups that fought to improve working conditions for women and children. She wrote newspaper and magazine articles.

In 1933, when Franklin D. Roosevelt became President, Eleanor—once the "ugly duckling," became the First Lady. President Roosevelt took office in the middle of the Great Depression. Millions of Americans were out of work. In America's cities, men and women stood in long lines, called "bread lines," waiting patiently for handouts of food. Many Americans lost their homes because they could no longer pay their bills. Farmers, unable to pay off their debts, had to give up farms that had been in the their families for generations. The Great Depression was like a dark cloud that had spread across the land.

People needed to feel hope—to feel that the people in high office cared about them. However, the President of the United States could not walk! Some twelve years before Franklin Roosevelt had been stricken with polio. Eleanor became the President's "eyes and ears." She went everywhere—she visited factories, schools, hospitals, prisons, shipyards, coal mines. She would talk to the people, ordinary people—and listen too. Then she would go back to the President to tell him what she saw, and what people said. Some Americans, by the way, felt it was wrong for her to do this since she was not in the government.

Eleanor also became a writer. A column she wrote appeared in 185 newspapers and many magazines carried articles written by her. She wrote eighteen books, most of them about her own life. Eleanor was the first wife of a President to hold regular meetings with news reporters, and to give talks on the radio. In 1945, she was selected as an American delegate to the United Nations.

What ever happened to "poor Eleanor"? A poll held in 1948 asked Americans, "Of all the women in the world, what woman do you admire the most?" When all the votes were counted, Eleanor Roosevelt, the girl who once was so afraid, was first.

Writing/Journal

1. WHAT'S THE BIG IDEA?

Copy out this story's most important message or main idea.

A. No one understands what fear is.

B. It is sometimes better to give in to a fear.

C. Different people have different fears.

D. It is better to conquer a fear instead of running away from it.

2. GET THE PICTURE

Here are eight scenes. Copy out the four scenes that best show Eleanor Roosevelt's life.

1. Little Eleanor laughing

2. Little Eleanor petting a dog

3. Little Eleanor swimming

4. Mrs. Roosevelt in the White House

5. Mrs. Roosevelt talking to a coal miner

6. Mrs. Roosevelt writing

7. Mrs. Roosevelt and the President walking together

8. Mrs. Roosevelt talking to reporters

3. WHO SAID THAT?

Here are six statements. Copy the three statements that Eleanor Roosevelt might have made.

1. "You must learn how to overcome your fear."

2. "Yes, I was a cheerful little girl."

3. "Oh, I don't want to talk to reporters."

4. "Diphtheria is a terrible disease."

5. "Oh, I rarely travel anywhere."

6. "Do not let people discourage you."

Let's Talk—Discussion Questions

4. THINK IT THROUGH

Give as many answers as you can for each question. Explain your answers.

— What are some ways people use today to overcome their fears?

— What might have happened to Eleanor if she had not overcome her fears?

— President Roosevelt told Americans during the Depression, "The only thing we have to fear, is fear itself?" What do you think he meant?

5. TAKE A SIDE

Here are two opinions on the same subject. Take one side or the other, and then give all the reasons you can for the side you take.

— "It is a good idea for the wife of the President to give her opinions and to get involved in the government."

— "The people do not elect the First Lady. She should keep out of anything to do with the government."

6. THEN AND NOW

— If a woman is elected President, what should be the role of her husband?

— President Roosevelt could not walk. Should someone be allowed to run for President today who has a serious health problem?

— There was no television when Roosevelt ran for office. How important is television in the election of a President today?

— Whether times were good or bad, Amerians have always kept faith in their democracy. What can today's Americans learn from this?

Cooperative Group Activities

7. IMAGINE

Imagine that you are a reporter at First Lady Eleanor Roosevelt's press conference. Ask her what advice she would give to a young boy or girl who is afraid and who is worried about many things.

8. LOOKING BACK

Select one of the events shown on the timeline for this story. Use other books or articles to gather more information about the event, and try to find out why the event was important. Present the information to the class or group.

1942

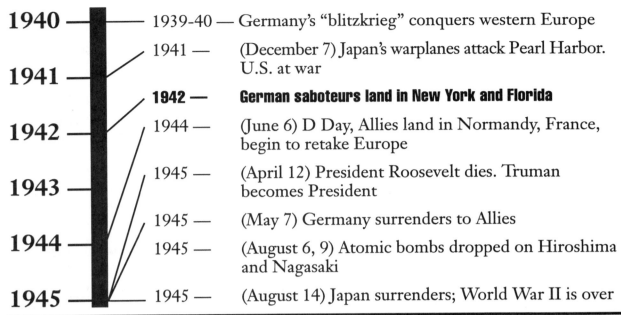

1940 —	1939-40 — Germany's "blitzkrieg" conquers western Europe
1941 —	1941 — (December 7) Japan's warplanes attack Pearl Harbor. U.S. at war
	1942 — German saboteurs land in New York and Florida
1942 —	1944 — (June 6) D Day, Allies land in Normandy, France, begin to retake Europe
1943 —	1945 — (April 12) President Roosevelt dies. Truman becomes President
1944 —	1945 — (May 7) Germany surrenders to Allies
	1945 — (August 6, 9) Atomic bombs dropped on Hiroshima and Nagasaki
1945 —	1945 — (August 14) Japan surrenders; World War II is over

What Else Was Happening?

On September 3, 1939, Americans were shocked by the news that the German army had invaded Poland. England and France immediately declared war on Germany. Twenty-one years after World War I ended, the second World War began. Germany quickly conquered almost all the countries in western Europe, including France.

While most Americans wanted to keep out of the war, their sympathies were with England and the democratic countries that Germany had conquered. Americans did not want to live in a world controlled by Adolph Hitler's Nazi Germany. The U.S. began shipping huge amounts of war supplies to England. When Germany made a surprise invasion of the Soviet Union, the U.S. shipped war goods to the Russians as well.

On December 7, 1941, Japan made a surprise attack on Pearl Harbor. This plunged the U.S. into World War II on the side of the Allies against the "Axis powers" of Japan, Germany, and Italy. Early in the war, Japan took over many important islands in the South-Pacific.

The Allies struck back by invading North Africa, then Italy, and finally, on June 6, 1944, France. The U.S. began retaking some of the islands in the Pacific. By early 1945, Germany had been beaten. Its cities lay in ruins. Japanese cities had also undergone many bombings. Germany surrendered in May, 1945. Japan surrendered three months later after atomic bombs had been dropped on the cities of Hiroshima and Nagasaki.

#10

The Secret Mission

On the overcast morning of May 28, 1942, the German submarine U-202 slipped out of its moorings in a harbor in southern France and headed for the open seas. As the submarine plowed through the cold Atlantic waters and the crew members went about their duties in the crowded quarters, four German soldiers sat cramped in the rear, deep in their own thoughts. If the soldiers appeared nervous, they had good reason. They were setting out on one of Germany's most secret missions during World War II.

By May, 1942, Germany had conquered Poland, Denmark, Norway, Belgium, Luxembourg, the Netherlands, and France. The victorious German Army was now pushing deep into the Soviet Union. Only England and the Soviet Union stood between Germany and a complete victory in Europe. In the meantime, the United States was sending huge amounts of war supplies to England and the Soviet Union to help them defeat Germany. The military leaders in Germany did not want to sit back while the U.S. kept sending these war supplies. They decided on a secret plan to stop the supplies right on American soil.

Germany had a school for sabotage located just outside of Berlin, the capital of Germany. Here, soldiers would be trained in how to set off explosive devices, and then they would be sent to America. There were plenty of experienced soldiers who knew how to set off explosives, but they would never do. Soldiers were needed who could speak good English and could pass themselves off as Americans. Before long, eight German soldiers were found who had lived in the United States and then returned to Germany. All of them spoke good English, and could pass for Americans. *Perfect!* One group of four would go by submarine to Florida. Another group would land in New York. One German soldier who had lived and worked as a waiter in New York was selected as the leader of the mission that would land in New York.

Experts trained the eight soldiers. They taught them how to knock out railroad tracks, blow up buildings, destroy bridges. They taught them every detail of how to set off explosions in factories making war supplies, then let them practice what they learned at nearby German factories. Most important of all, each man had a "cover" so that he could pass himself off as an American. They were given draft cards, ration books, driver's licenses—everything to make them appear to be Americans. Each man memorized a made-up history of himself in America. They read the latest American newspapers and magazines. Above all, the ex-

Courtesy, Library of Congress

Not even saboteurs could stop the huge amount of war goods coming from America.

perts pounded at them over and over again, there was to be no slip up if they wanted to pass as Americans...

Sixteen days after it had left France, the German submarine stopped its engines and broke the ocean surface one-half mile off the coast of Long Island, New York. It was a few minutes after midnight. The submarine captain—pleased by the heavy mist that hung over the area—shook each soldier's hand, wished them well, and then helped them board a rubber boat inflated with air.

One hour later the four German sabo-teurs stood on the sandy shore of Long Island congratulating each other on how smoothly everything had gone. They changed out of their soaking German uniforms and into American type civilian clothes, then buried the uniforms and the deflated boat in the sand along with four heavy boxes. *So far, so good...*

About the same time the Germans were wading ashore, a U.S. Coast Guard rookie was starting his dreary after-midnight patrol. Flashlight in hand, he walked alone along the deserted beach. As usual, the heavy fog kept him from seeing too far ahead, but now, as he rounded a sand dune, he spotted the unmistakable figure of a man.

"Who's there?" He called out. His flashlight's beam hit the figure.

"I'm George Davis," the leader of the group called back. "We're fishermen. We've had a little bad luck and we ran aground." His voice was calm. *There was to be no slip up.*

The sailor had no reason to doubt the story; it was not unusual for fishermen to be out this late in warm weather. As the sailor drew closer, he caught sight of three other figures a few yards back. He aimed the flashlight at the other three men. The sudden flash of light caught one of the soldiers by surprise. Startled, without thinking and despite all the training in how to act like an American, he muttered something—in German!

The leader of the group fumed. After all the work at the sabotage school, one of the men had let his German slip out. The leader looked to see if the American had heard it. If he had, he gave no hint of it—though it was hard to tell in the darkness.

The American sailor cleared his throat, "Why don't you guys just come back to the Coast Guard base with me and—" The leader's heart stopped. *Did the American sailor know? Was the plan ruined by one stupid slip?* The leader reached into his pocket.

"Look," he stared at the young Coast Guardsman and pulled out some tens and twenties. "Here's three hundred dollars. Take it. Forget everything you've seen here." It was a crazy thing to do, and the leader knew it, but he felt he had to do something. The Coast Guardsmen reached out, took the money and left. The Germans were left to wonder if he would really forget the matter.

"Let's get out of here," the leader shouted to the others.

The four saboteurs took a train to New York City where they registered at a hotel. Meantime, the sailor reported what had happened as soon as he got back to his base. The Coast Guard was soon digging up the boxes the saboteurs had buried. In the boxes they found what looked like pieces of coal but were really bombs that could be used to destroy factories that burned coal. They also found a large supply of time bombs.

Within six days, all the saboteurs, including the ones who landed in Florida, were rounded up, and placed in jail. American newspapers screamed the news: Eight saboteurs caught on American soil. Explosives found. Fake identification uncovered.

One slip, one moment of forgetfulness, and it was all over.

The saboteurs certainly would have done some harm. However, even if they had not been caught, they could never have stopped the huge amount of war materials. America had shifted from manufacturing such things as autos and washing machines to producing tanks and airplanes. As the world's greatest industrial nation, the U.S. was producing and shipping an overwhelming amount of war supplies. Two years later, on June 6, 1944, the greatest armada the world had ever seen, sailed across the English Channel. Allied troops, including many Americans, landed in France and began the push to reconquer western Europe. The giant flow of American supplies would continue until Germany's surrender on May 7, 1945.

Writing/Journal Activities

1. WHAT'S THE BIG IDEA?

Copy out this story's most important message or main idea.

A. Sabotage is dangerous work.

B. Keep your mind on what you are doing.

C. Submarines are important in wartime.

D. Training is important in anything you do.

2. GET THE PICTURE

Here are eight scenes that an artist might have painted. Copy out the four scenes that best describe this story.

1. a submarine
2. U.S. factories
3. a French sailor
4. A Japanese sailor
5. small explosive devices
6. a shining flashlight
7. a television set
8. an airplane in the sky

3. WHO SAID THAT?

Here are six statements. Copy the three statements that a saboteur in the story might have made.

1. "We received a lot of training."
2. "We will try to damage some U.S. factories."
3. "We want people to think we are French."
4. "Our mission was a great success."
5. "We want to stop the U.S. war shipments."
6. "We tried to bribe someone and it worked."

Let's Talk—Discussion Activities

4. THINK IT THROUGH

Give as many answers as you can for each question.

— Some people say that it is all right to do anything in a war. Do you agree or disagree. Explain.

— Why were the American factories so important?

5. TAKE A SIDE

Here are two opinions on the same subject. Take one side or the other, and then give all the reasons you can for the side you take.

— "In time of war, people in a democracy should be willing to give up many of their freedoms."

— "There should never be a time when the people in a democracy have to give up any freedoms."

6. THEN AND NOW

— Name some freedoms Americans have today that they had to give up during World War II.

— What weapons do armies and navies have today that they did not have in World War II?

Cooperative Group Activities

7. IMAGINE

The young sailor in the story refused to be bribed. Imagine someone offered you a million dollars to be disloyal to your country. Explain what you would do and say.

8. A LOOK BACK

Select one of the events shown on the timeline for this story. Use other books or articles to gather more information about the event, and try to find out why the event was important. Present the information to the class or group.

1955

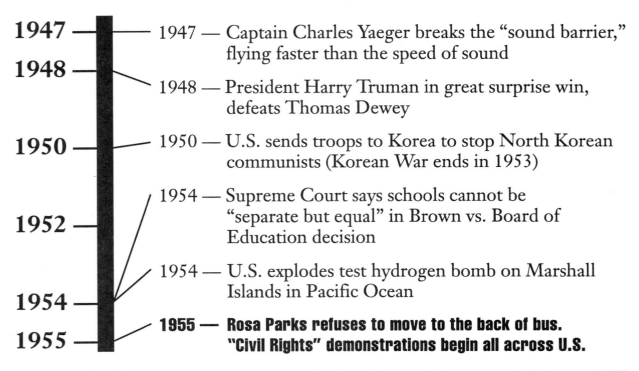

1947 — Captain Charles Yaeger breaks the "sound barrier," flying faster than the speed of sound

1948 — President Harry Truman in great surprise win, defeats Thomas Dewey

1950 — U.S. sends troops to Korea to stop North Korean communists (Korean War ends in 1953)

1954 — Supreme Court says schools cannot be "separate but equal" in Brown vs. Board of Education decision

1954 — U.S. explodes test hydrogen bomb on Marshall Islands in Pacific Ocean

1955 — Rosa Parks refuses to move to the back of bus. "Civil Rights" demonstrations begin all across U.S.

What Else Was Happening?

The U.S. became a world leader after World War II. To keep communism from spreading, the U.S. and the countries in western Europe agreed to protect each other from an attack by the Soviet Union. Under the Marshall Plan, the U.S. also sent money and supplies to help Europeans rebuild their war-torn cities. When communist North Korea invaded South Korea in 1950, President Truman ordered American troops to help the South Koreans. After three years of war, the North Koreans agreed to stop fighting. Americans believed their action in Korea helped stop the spread of communism in Asia.

During the 1950's African Americans began what was called the "Civil Rights Movement," demanding equal rights for all Americans. There were marches, demonstrations, boycotts, and sit-ins to point up the need for change. In response, Congress passed the Civil Rights Act in 1957 that aimed at giving equal rights to all Americans.

#11
Enough!

The bus driver turned around and stared at the middle-aged woman seated five rows behind him.

"I said to get up and move back," he grumbled.

When the woman made no effort to move, the driver pulled the bus to the side of the road, stood up, and pushed his way down the aisle to where the woman was seated.

"You hear me,"—he flung the words as if he were throwing rocks at her—"I said move back."

The usual noisy chatter of the people on the bus grew suddenly—strangely—silent. A few riders turned around or stood up. *What was going on?*

"I'm telling you for the last time,"—the driver towered over her now—"move to the back of the bus like you are supposed to."

Rosa Parks—for that was the middle-aged woman's name—stared out the window at Montgomery's evening traffic. Ordinarily Rosa Parks would have done exactly what the driver told her to do. She was neither ornery nor stubborn. And she certainly knew the law about segregating African Americans from whites in Montgomery, Alabama. The neatly printed sign on the first four rows of the bus proclaimed, "Whites Only." As an African American she could sit in the fifth row of the bus, but only so long as there were empty seats in those first four rows. When she got on the bus, the front rows were empty. Now they were full, and two white men had just come aboard. Rosa Parks would have to give up her seat. That was the law.

Ordinarily Rosa would have done what she was supposed to do. She always had before. But this late afternoon she was tired—bone tired—after a full day of sewing at the department store where she worked. Her feet ached, her fingers felt sore, and the bagful of groceries she had brought on the bus weighed heavily on her arms. What's more, she would have to walk a good few blocks after she got off the bus. No, she was just too tired to get up and stand.

Even after the bus driver warned her that he was going to call the police, Rosa remained quietly seated. Rosa Parks would never know for certain why she chose just that moment to do what she did. After all, she had grown up in the South; she knew she was supposed to obey the "Jim Crow" laws. "Jim Crow" was the name of the laws and regulations that kept African Americans separated from white

Courtesy, The Bettmann Archive

Even after the bus driver warned her, Rosa Parks remained seated.

Rosa Parks had gone along with the "Jim Crow" rules before. What was different this time? Was she really just tired, or was there something inside of her that said, "Enough. I have had enough"?

Not even Rosa Parks knew for certain...

Rosa was arrested, charged with breaking the law, and fined ten dollars plus four dollars for court costs. That should have ended things right there. But this was December, 1955, and throughout the 1950's things were beginning to stir. Other Americans were beginning to think "enough" too, and Rosa Parks, instead of becoming a tired lady who broke the law and paid fourteen dollars, became the center of a gathering storm. The storm would rage through the South first, but the violent winds of unrest were soon felt all across the land.

The leaders of the African American community had been trying to change the bus rules in Montgomery for a long time, but they had always failed. With the arrest of Rosa Parks, they were ready to try again. They hit upon a plan: they would boycott, that is, refuse to use, the buses. The cry went out—at church meetings, on street corners, in stores, on printed flyers: "Do not ride the buses in Montgomery until the bus companies treat us fairly and with dignity."

Now, it was one thing to urge the African American people not to ride the buses, but it would be quite another thing to carry it out. How would African American people get to work and back each day? And how would they have money for food and rent if they did not take the bus to work?

people in restaurants, in theaters, at schools, at drinking fountains—and on buses.

"Jim Crow" got its name from a white actor in the 1830's who blackened his face and hands, shuffled about the stage, and poked fun at African American people. Even though the Civil War ended in 1865, it was not until about 1900 that "Jim Crow" laws were passed in the Southern states. And the law in Alabama said that African Americans and whites were to be separated on the bus.

Other bus boycotts had been tried and had failed. But this time, something about the way Rosa Parks had stood up, something about the 1950's, something about the way an unknown twenty-six year old minister named Martin Luther King Jr. spoke at gatherings, something inside of other Americans said "it was time." And so, African Americans went about finding other ways to get to work. They walked, they took African American owned taxis that charged ten cents a ride, they shared rides in autos, they climbed aboard horse drawn buggies, they even took mules. They took everything and anything—except buses. The African American leaders had hope that as much as sixty percent of the African Americans would stay off the buses. In fact just about every single African American person in Montgomery refused to ride a bus.

But the bus boycott was only half of the story. Rosa Parks had started something else. Yes, the law of Alabama declared that African Americans were to be separated from whites, but what about the United States Constitution? *Didn't the Constitution say that citizens were to be treated as equals? Wasn't the law in Alabama doing something that the Constitution said it could not do?* Lawyers appealed the conviction of Rosa Parks to the United States Supreme Court. When the case came before the Court, the Supreme Court Justices quickly decided that a state could not make laws that separated one group of Americans from another group of Americans. These laws, the Court said, were against what the Constitution said.

As Rosa Parks quietly awaited the arrival of a police officer that December evening in 1955, she had little idea of what she was starting. Across the land, boycotts, marches, meetings, and every kind of protesting would make the headlines in the 1950's and into the 1960's in the struggle for equal rights. In 1957 the U.S. Congress would pass the Civil Rights law aimed at giving equal rights to all Americans. Rosa Parks had taken a single brick from the "Jim Crow" wall, and watched the wall crack, and then crumble to the ground.

Writing/Journal Activities

1. THE STORY

Make up three good questions about this story. Write the answers after each question.

2. WHAT'S THE QUESTION?

Here are six questions a reporter might have asked Rosa Parks. Copy out what you consider to be the three most important questions.

1. "How old were you when this happened?"

2. "Did you feel proud or ashamed of what you did?"

3. "How did your friends and neighbors feel about what you did?"

4. "What kind of clothes were you wearing that day?"

5. "Why did you decide not to move on the bus?"

6. "How long did it take before the police arrived?"

3. FIND THE HEADLINE

Here are three newspaper headlines. Copy the one headline that best tells the main idea of the story.

1. Arrest of Woman Leads to Changes in the Law

2. Bus Driver Has Woman Arrested

3. People Protest Arrest of Woman

4. TAKE IT OR LEAVE IT

Here are eight words that might be used to describe someone. Copy out the four words that best describe Rosa Parks.

1. brave	2. persevering	3. timid
4. strong-willed	5. determined	6. weak
7. hesitant	8. cowardly	

11

Let's Talk—Discussion Activities

5. THINK IT THROUGH

Give as many answers as you can for each question.

— Give an example of someone today who stands up for what he or she believes is right.

— Can you respect someone who stands up for what he or she thinks is right, even if you do not agree with the person? Explain.

— The bus boycott hurt the bus company. How could a boycott hurt other businesses as well?

6. TAKE A SIDE

Here are two opinions on the same subject. Take one side or the other, and then give all the reasons you can for the side you take.

— "It is wrong to break a law. Instead, if you want a law changed, write letters to the people who make the laws."

— "Sometimes, you have to break the law in order to get the law changed."

Cooperative Group Activities

7. IMAGINE

Make up the front page of a newspaper that might have been published in 1955. Have stories that describe what happened in Montgomery, Alabama.

8. LOOK BACK

Select one of the events shown on the timeline for this story. Use other books or articles to gather more information about the event, and try to find out why the event was important. Present the information to the class or group.

1966

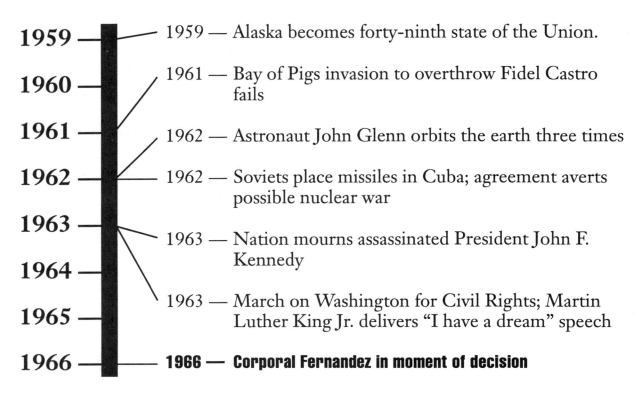

1959	1959 — Alaska becomes forty-ninth state of the Union.
1960	1961 — Bay of Pigs invasion to overthrow Fidel Castro fails
1961	1962 — Astronaut John Glenn orbits the earth three times
1962	1962 — Soviets place missiles in Cuba; agreement averts possible nuclear war
1963	1963 — Nation mourns assassinated President John F. Kennedy
1964	
1965	1963 — March on Washington for Civil Rights; Martin Luther King Jr. delivers "I have a dream" speech
1966	**1966 — Corporal Fernandez in moment of decision**

What Else Was Happening?

In the 1960's the U.S. began sending soldiers to help the South Vietnamese fight the communists coming from North Vietnam. Each year, more soldiers were sent until by the early 1970's almost half a million American soldiers were in Vietnam. Many Americans felt it was wrong for U.S. soldiers to be fighting there. Many other Americans believed that it was right because this was a way America could stop the spread of communism. The war did not end until 1973. By then more than 50 thousand Americans had died, 100 billion dollars had been spent, and the North Vietnamese had not been stopped. Not since the Civil war, had Americans been so divided by a war.

#12

Moment of Decision

Danny Fernandez had been on patrols in Vietnam before, but never had he faced such intense enemy fire. Automatic and rifle fire seemed to be coming from every direction. He was not surprised then, when his sergeant gave the order for the advance patrol to move back. Fernandez gripped his rifle tightly as he and the rest of the soldiers in the squad stumbled back, away from the heavy enemy fire. The men did not stop until they reached a small clearing in the brush. Relieved and breathing a little easier, Fernandez and the others were catching their breaths when the sergeant burst into the clearing. He grunted angrily as he spoke.

One of the men in the squad had been hit. He was lying out there somewhere, wounded. "We need volunteers to pick him up and bring him back," the sergeant grumbled. "Who wants to go?"

Fernandez and two others agreed to go back. A short time later, the four soldiers were working their way back towards their old position, the sergeant leading the way. The sounds of enemy fire grew louder with each step. Suddenly the sergeant stopped in his tracks and signaled with his left arm—the wounded soldier lay just ahead. The sergeant crept forward, Fernandez trailing a few feet behind, with the other two volunteers just behind him. A sudden burst of machine gun fire—closer than the other battle noises—ripped the air. The sergeant let out a soft moan and dropped to the ground. Fernandez motioned the other two men to move forward. There would be two wounded soldiers to take back now.

Fernandez crawled slowly towards the sergeant. The machine gun fire had smashed the sergeant's right knee. Fernandez reached for his first aid kit, then dropped his head and hugged the ground as a new burst of fire erupted. He lifted his head again in time to see something bounce along the ground and come to rest about a foot away from the sergeant. Fernandez's heart seemed to stop. He recognized the unmistakable outline of an enemy grenade.

That grenade will blow in seconds. There is no time to warn the sergeant and get him out, no time to tell the others, no time to...

Twenty-one year old Daniel Fernandez left his home in Albuquerque, New Mexico to enlist in the U.S. Army in 1965. A year later, Specialist Fourth Class Daniel Fernandez of the 25th Infantry landed in South Vietnam. About this time, the United

Courtesy, George Rollins

Inscribed on the black granite are the names of 57,792 Americans killed or missing.

States was sending troops to South Vietnam to stop communist soldiers who were taking over many of the villages there. The U.S. government believed that unless the communists were stopped, they would take over South Vietnam and then would go on to conquer neighboring countries in Asia.

At first, most Americans agreed with their government, but as the war dragged on, and more and more soldiers were killed or wounded, some Americans began to question why we were fighting in Vietnam. These American protested the war by marching in the streets or holding meetings at colleges. As more and more American troops were sent,

and more of them were killed, wounded, or captured, the protests grew larger. At the same time, many other Americans felt it was important to keep communism from spreading all over Asia. Not since the Civil War a 100 years before had Americans been so divided in a time of war.

Fernandez crouched in his position. At that instant the arguing, the protesting back in the United States meant nothing to him. His wounded sergeant lay in front, the two other volunteers were just behind. And none of them saw the grenade. It was going to deto- nate in a second; the deadly bits of metal would explode in every directions. *What do I do now?* Danny Fernandez leaped over the sergeant, and landed squarely on the grenade. He smothered the grenade with his chest— and waited...

The argument and protesting over whether or not the United States soldiers should continue fighting in Vietnam went on until 1975 when the last U.S. troops left South Vietnam. Even after the war, people felt torn apart by whether or not the war was right. Returning soldiers in other wars were greeted as heroes. When the soldiers came back from Vietnam, there were no parades, no kind words, no praise. It seemed as though the country did not appreciate the sacrifices the service men and women in Vietnam had made.

A few years later, some Americans began to realize that the veterans of Vietnam, like the veterans before them, should be honored and respected for the sacrifices they had made. It was time to heal the wounds that had so divided the country. In November of 1982 a five day salute was held in Washington D.C. to honor the Vietnam veterans. While fifteen thousand former service men and women marched, huge crowds cheered. On the last day of the celebrations, on November 13, 1982, a Vietnam Veterans Memorial was unveiled and dedicated. The memorial was a 500 foot long V-shaped black wall of granite. Inscribed on the black granite were the names of the 57,792 Americans killed or missing in Vietnam.

At first, Americans complained that the monument was too simple and too bare to serve as a symbol of honor for our service- men. Then, as thousands of people streamed past the memorial over the next few months a strange thing began to happen. The visitors seemed overwhelmed. Some stood in rever- ent silence; others sought out the name of a loved one, then traced their fingers lovingly over it; a few spread bits of papers over names, then ran pencils back and forth until the names appeared on the papers. Many stood in silent thought staring at the names.

Years have passed since Daniel Fernandez hurled himself over his sergeant that February day in 1966. He received the Congres- sional Medal of Honor for action "above and beyond the call of duty" for what he did that day. The medal—the highest and rarest award a serviceman can receive—is not worn like other medals, but is held on a blue sash that hangs from the neck. However, Fernandez never draped his Medal of Honor about his neck. One of the names inscribed on the dark marble of the Vietnam Veterans Memorial reads: Daniel Fernandez.

Writing/Journal Activities

1. THE STORY

Make up three good questions about this story. Write the answers after each question.

2. WHAT'S THE QUESTION?

Here are six questions a reporter might have asked a soldier fighting in Vietnam. Copy out what you consider the three most important questions.

1. "Why are you fighting in Vietnam?"

2. "What part of the U.S. are you from?"

3. "What are some hardships you face?"

4. "How many meals do you have in a day?"

5. "Should U.S. soldiers keep fighting in Vietnam or should they leave?"

6. "What kind of uniform do you wear?"

3. FIND THE HEADLINE

Here are three newspaper headlines. Copy the one headline that best tells the main idea of the story.

1. Vietnam War Rages On

2. America Finally Honors Its Vietnam Heroes

3. Veterans of War Suffer Many Hardships

4. SEARCH AND FIND

Find the word (or words) closest to the meaning of the underlined word in each sentence. Then copy the sentence, using that word (or words) in place of the underlined word.

1. The enemy fire aimed at them was <u>intense</u>.
   weak   powerful   scattered   not regular

2. Fernandez was glad when they reached the <u>clearing</u>.
   open space   quiet place   warm space   friendly place

3. He knew the grenade would <u>detonate</u>.
   do damage   cause injuries   block things out   explode

4. The Vietnam monument, dedicated to those who died, was <u>unveiled</u> in 1982
   uncovered   dedicated   covered   sealed

5. Visitors to the monument were <u>overwhelmed</u>.
   overcome   shocked   surprised   startled

6. Some stood in <u>reverent</u> silence.
   polite   cordial   lasting   respectful

Let's Talk—Discussion Activities

5. THINK IT THROUGH

Give as many answers as you can for each question.

— Why do you think Fernandez did what he did? Do you think you could have done the same thing?

— Are people braver in time of war than they are during peacetime? Explain.

— Fernandez was a hero. Who are some of our heroes today?

6. TAKE A SIDE

Here are two opinions on the same subject. Take one side or the other, and then give all the reasons you can for the side you take.

— "Once the U.S. gets into a war, you should be loyal, and not protest."

— "If I think the war is wrong, it is all right for me to protest."

Cooperative Group Activities

7. IMAGINE

Select three or more qualities that you think a hero is likely to have; select three or more qualities that you think a hero is not likely to have.

Imagine medals were given to people who made sacrifces in their personal lives. Describe a time you, or someone you knew, acted in a heroic manner to earn a medal.

8. LOOK BACK

Select one of the events shown on the timeline for this story. Use other books or articles to gather more information about the event, and try to find out why the event was important. Present the information to the class or group.

1969

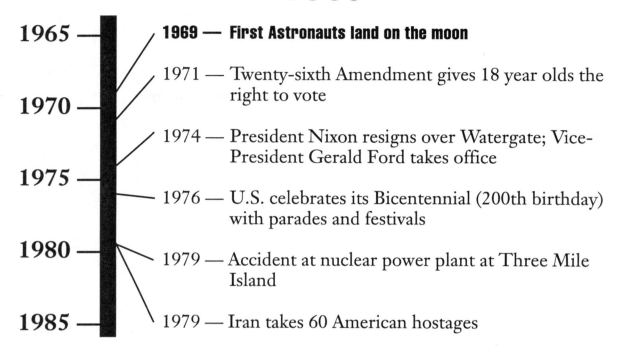

1965

1970

1975

1980

1985

1969 — First Astronauts land on the moon

1971 — Twenty-sixth Amendment gives 18 year olds the right to vote

1974 — President Nixon resigns over Watergate; Vice-President Gerald Ford takes office

1976 — U.S. celebrates its Bicentennial (200th birthday) with parades and festivals

1979 — Accident at nuclear power plant at Three Mile Island

1979 — Iran takes 60 American hostages

What Else Was Happening?

Many people and organizations became concerned about protecting the environment during the 1970's. Americans wanted air free of health hazards, and its rivers, lakes, and ocean water free of "pollutants." The first government agency to protect the environment was set up in 1970. In 1979 an accident at a nuclear power plant at Three Mile Island released a small amount of radio-active steam. No lives were lost and the damage was repaired, but Americans wanted to be certain that other atomic energy plants would remain safe.

Though eighteen year olds could be drafted to fight in a war, they could not vote until the age of 21. The Twenty-Sixth Amendment was added to the Constitution in 1971. This amendment gave 18 year olds the right to vote.

#13

Danger Ahead!

As the moon landing craft descended, a tense Neil Armstrong stared out the window at the rugged surface of the moon some 200 feet below. Suddenly, Armstrong's heartbeat raced from a calm 60 beats per minute to a pounding 177 beats—and with good reason. The lunar (moon) landing craft's automatic pilot was taking astronauts Neil Armstrong and Edwin Aldrin straight towards a moon crater the size of a football field. Boulders and rocks lay scattered all over the crater! If the landing craft stayed on course, it would smash into the boulders. Even if, by some miracle, it missed all of the boulders, the lunar craft would land at an angle. Such an angle landing would make it impossible to take off later, and the two astronauts would be stranded on the moon forever.

Armstrong had to take some quick action or man's first landing on the moon would be a disaster. He glanced at the array of instruments if front of him. He could flip some switches and shoot the spacecraft up again—but if he did, he would probably not have enough fuel left to try to land on the moon again. Or, he could use up precious fuel to guide the craft towards a safer spot—but would this maneuver leave enough fuel for him to take off later? All of these thoughts raced through Armstrong's mind as the craft drew closer and closer to the moon.

Up to now—ever since takeoff—the flight had been going so well. Four days before, on Wednesday morning, July 16, 1969, astronauts Neil Armstrong, Buzz Aldrin, Jr., and Michael Collins sat manning the controls aboard Apollo 11 on earth listening to the Houston Control count-down. "...five, four, three, two, one, zero, engines are running. Lift-off. We have a lift-off." At the end of the countdown, huge, orange-tinged flames burst from the tail of the 363 foot silvery Saturn rocket. The Appollo 11 pushed skyward, and the three brave astronauts were on their way—for the first try ever to reach the moon. Two minutes later, the engines of the first stage (the back section) of the spacecraft were cut off. Then the second stage was separated, and the third stage ignited, boosting the spacecraft's speed to 17,432 miles per hour. The added speed placed the spacecraft into orbit around the earth. Halfway through its second orbit, the third stage was ignited again. The new burst shot the spacecraft's speed to 24,200 miles per hour. At that speed,

Courtesy, National Aeronautics and Space Administration

"The surface is fine and powdery."

the spacecraft broke away from the earth's orbit and headed towards the moon.

Everything was going well.

A quarter of a million miles and four days later, the spacecraft tumbled through space and passed over the moon. At this point, huge rocket engines slowed the spacecraft enough for the moon's gravity to pull the craft into the moon's orbit. The astronauts maneuvered the craft closer to the moon's surface. Armstrong and Aldrin crawled through a tunnel into the landing module and took their places at the controls. They separated the landing module from the Apollo 11, and headed for the moon's surface. Meantime, the Apollo 11, with Collins still aboard, continued to circle the moon.

All seemed to be going well. Down and down the landing craft went. Two thousand feet...one thousand...five hundred...and then the startling realization that all was not well—that they were headed towards a crater filled with boulders!

Neil Armstrong was used to making tough, dangerous decisions. He had flown 78 combat missions off aircraft carriers during the Korean war. He had pushed an experimental plane to a top speed of 4,000 miles an hour. And once he had made an emergency splash down in the Pacific when his spacecraft had suddenly tumbled out of control. No, making quick emergency decisions was not new to Armstrong.

Four hundred feet from the surface of the moon, Armstrong flipped a switch that took the craft off automatic pilot. He was now in complete control. He veered the craft off to the side away from the crater—to a safe lunar landing!

Some hours later, a white clad figure slowly climbed down the ladder of the space ship. Armstrong placed his left foot on the fine grained surface of the moon. "This is one small step for a man, one giant leap for mankind," he said.

Minutes later, fellow-astronaut Edwin Aldrin joined Armstrong, and together they set up television cameras to beam their movements back to earth. Moving about in the harsh light of the lunar morning they reported—"The surface is fine and powdery." Then, thanks to the moon's lesser gravity pull, they jumped and loped across the barren moon landscape. Before long, the serious work began—they scooped up rocks, snapped photos, probed the soil, and set in motion many types of experiments.

Four days later, the three weary astronauts made a safe landing back on earth. For centuries, men and women had dreamed of going to the moon. On a July day in 1969—at long last—the dream of reaching the moon and returning to earth became real.

Writing/Journal Activities

1. THE STORY

Make up three good questions about this story. Write the answers after each question.

2. WHAT'S THE QUESTION?

Here are six questions a reporter might have asked the astronauts who went to the moon. Copy out what you consider the three most important questions.

1. "Why should the U.S. spend so much money going to the moon?"

2. "Did you feel lonely during your trip to the moon?"

3. "What were some of the scientific experiments you performed?"

4. "What do you think made the mission successful?"

5. "How old are you?"

6. "What did people say to you when you returned?"

3. FIND THE HEADLINE

Here are three newspaper headlines. Copy out the one headline that best tells the main idea of the story.

1. First Landing on the Moon Succeeds

2. Astronaut Armstrong Averts Danger in Landing

3. Astronauts Find Less Gravity on the Moon

4. SEARCH AND FIND

Find the word (or words) closest to the meaning of the underlined word in each sentence. Then copy the sentence, using that word (or words) in place of the underlined word.

1. The moon landing craft <u>descended</u>.
   came down   came down slowly   came down quickly   went up

2. The astronauts might be <u>stranded</u> on the moon.
   without food   marooned   without water   rescued

3. They <u>maneuvered</u> the space craft close to the moon.
   flew   guided   shot   blasted

4. The spaceship was headed for a <u>crater</u>.
   a small mountain   a deep gully   a rounded hole in the ground   a hill

13

5. He had flown many times under <u>combat</u> conditions.
war   clouded   secret   special

6. The spaceship <u>veered</u> sharply to the left.
shook   jerked   turned   jolted

Let's Talk—Discussion Activities

5. THINK IT THROUGH

Give as many answers as you can for each question

— Why are people so interested in the unknown?

— Would you be willing to go as a passenger on the next space flight? Explain why or why not.

6. TAKE A SIDE

Here are two opinions on the same subject. Take one side or the other, and then give all the reasons you can for the side you take.

—"The United States should continue sending astronauts into space."

—"The space program is a waste of money. We should spend the money on other, more important things."

Cooperative Group Activities

7. IMAGINE

Imagine that you are a modern day scientist. Write a letter to a scientist who lived on earth 200 years ago. Tell about five or more scientific inventions that might surprise the old scientist.

8. A LOOK BACK

Select one of the events shown on the timeline for this story. Use other books or articles to gather more information about the event, and try to find out why the event was important. Present the information to the class or group.

1988

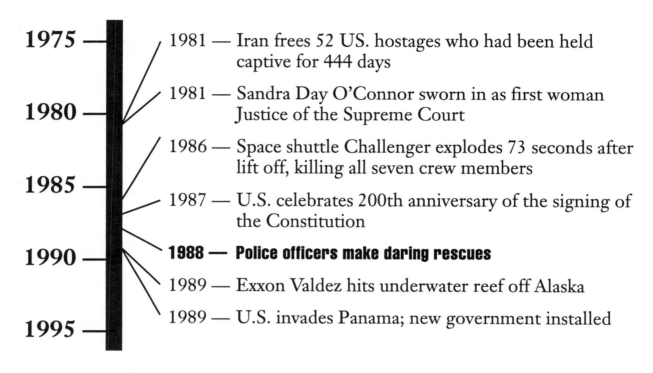

1975

1980

1985

1990

1995

1981 — Iran frees 52 U.S. hostages who had been held captive for 444 days

1981 — Sandra Day O'Connor sworn in as first woman Justice of the Supreme Court

1986 — Space shuttle Challenger explodes 73 seconds after lift off, killing all seven crew members

1987 — U.S. celebrates 200th anniversary of the signing of the Constitution

1988 — Police officers make daring rescues

1989 — Exxon Valdez hits underwater reef off Alaska

1989 — U.S. invades Panama; new government installed

What Else Was Happening?

The explosion of the space shuttle Challenger shortly after take-off shocked the millions of Americans who were watching on television in 1986. All seven on board the Challenger were killed. Some Americans wondered whether or not the space program should be continued, but later space flights were successful. A different kind of disaster took place in 1989 when a tanker filled with oil hit a reef off Alaska. Thousands of gallons of oil spilled into the sea and damaged much of the wildlife in the area. It was the worst tanker spill in U.S. history.

America celebrated the two-hundredth anniversary of the signing of the Constitution in 1989. The Constitution remains a remarkable plan for running the government. It allows Americans to govern themselves as a free people, and it also protects their rights and liberties.

#14

To Protect and Serve

As cities grew more crowded during the 1980's, Americans became more concerned about crime. Movies, television news, and television programs that showed policemen shooting guns or fighting became very popular. Police officers, however, pointed out there was another side to their work—a side that does not just involve shooting and fighting, but doing things to protect and serve the people. Many police departments present Medal of Valor awards each year to police officers whose outstanding acts of bravery in the face of danger are examples of how the police protect and serve the people. Sometimes, this means using a weapon, but more often it means doing the bravest thing any man or woman can be called upon to do. What one San Diego police officer did on an October morning in 1988 is one example...

Police Officer Castellini gripped the steering wheel tightly, and glanced at the speedometer as the arrow passed 70 miles per hour. A moment before, he had seen a stolen black Nissan 280Z on the freeway and had called for help on his car radio. Now, he was racing through the darkness this early October morning in 1988, keeping his eyes on the stolen car's rear red lights.

As Castellini drew closer, the lights of the car up ahead suddenly disappeared! The driver of the other car had seen the black and white car following him, and had turned off his lights. Castellini heard the roar of the car's engine as it sped away in the darkness. He decided not to race after the speeding car—it was too dangerous. Castellini let up on the gas pedal. He knew this part of the freeway through San Diego well; he would try to follow at a safe speed.

There were no other cars on the freeway this early in the morning. And so, there were no headlights to show the thief where the roadway curves began or ended. Castellini was reporting what was happening on his car radio when he stopped in the middle of a sentence. The horrible thumping noise that a car makes when it smashes against a freeway barrier resounded across the freeway. As Castellini drove closer he saw the shadowy outline of a car in the darkness bounce off the freeway barrier, and roll completely over. The screeching noise of metal against concrete ripped Castellini's ears as the car slid—wheels up—all the way across the freeway. Finally, its wheels still whirling up at the early morning sky, the car came to a stop.

Castellini clicked the switch on his car radio, shouted for help, then braked his black and white to a stop. He jumped out. Black smoke was pouring out of the stolen car's engine, and Castellini caught the smell of gasoline.

"Help me," A man's voice shrieked from inside the car. "Somebody help me. I can't get out!"

Through the years the goal remains—Protect and Serve

Castellini reassured the man that help was on the way. He heard police and fire sirens off in the distance. "Help is on the way," he shouted.

"I don't want to burn up," the driver pleaded.

"You'll be all right," Castellini answered. "They'll be here in a few minutes." Black smoke kept pouring from the engine and the smell of gasoline was everywhere. He thought: *a few minutes may be too long to wait..*

The back window of the stolen car was smashed in. Castellini quickly knocked away the remaining bits of glass, and crawled into the back of the car. Inside the smell of the gasoline grew stronger. The gasoline tank had split open. The car was sitting at a crazy angle so that gasoline was dripping all over the car! The driver was soaked from head to foot.

Police Officer Castellini reached over the front seat and grabbed the driver under his arms. He tugged, then tugged again, but the driver could not be budged. Castellini looked down. Part of the upside down car had landed on top of the thief's left foot. There was no way the officer could loosen the foot by himself.

By now Castellini's own shirt and pants were soaked with gasoline. This thing can blow any minute, he thought. Still, he kept his grip on the driver, and kept telling the man trapped in the car, "Don't worry. Everything is going to be all right." Finally, Castellini heard the sound of two police cars screeching to a stop, and policemen running towards them.

"I got a man pinned in here," he shouted. "Get the left side of this car up—quick."

Castellini breathed a sigh of relief as he felt the car being lifted up. He moved the driver's leg until it came free, then quickly dragged the screaming man through the window to safety.

Minutes later Castellini stood watching as the firemen smothered the car in foam, and washed away the gasoline. Officer Castellini had known all along just how dangerous it was to go inside that car—but he had gone in just the same. Later, someone told Castellini that it seemed strange for a policeman to risk his life to save a thief. Castellini just shrugged his shoulders. After, all it was just part of his job as a policeman.

#14

In Des Moines, Iowa, some 1500 miles away, on a warm spring morning in the same year, six year old Joey was running along a pond's "black dirt," as Joey called it. The "black dirt" was not dirt at all, but a thin layer of darkened ice. The small boy ran a few more steps, then—too late—he felt himself falling through the ice and into the freezing waters below.

Joey's eight year old brother and an eight year old friend rushed to the edge of the pond. They held out sticks for Joey to grab, but Joey was too frightened to do what he was told. The boys moved to the edge of the pool, and moments later all three were struggling to keep their heads above the water. Somehow Joey manage to grab onto his brother's shirt as the two older boys started to pull themselves onto a large chunk of ice. As they climbed on the ice however, Joey's fingers lost their grip. He slipped beneath the surface and out of sight.

A hundred feet from the pond, a man staring out his kitchen window heard the shouts of help. He dialed 911...

Officer Gary Cowger was cruising in an unmarked police car just a few blocks from the pond when the news crackled over the radio. He raced to the scene, then skidded to a stop at the pond's edge. Because Cowger was not in his regular patrol car, he had no rescue equipment. "Stay calm," he shouted to the boys. Cowger braced his body for the jolt of cold—then jumped in and waded towards the boys. After a few steps, the water was over his head!

Cowger heard two more police cars pull up and turned in time to see two officers holding out a rope for him. He quickly turned back, wrapped the rope about his waist, and—with the two officers holding onto the end of the rope—swam towards the chuck of ice. Despite the bitter cold, he kept up his strong, steady stroking motions.

Halfway there, he heard the officers on shore shout something. Cowger stared through the cold, dark, murky waters at what looked like a "bundle." Cowger's heart sank. *It's a child!* He grabbed the unconscious small boy, rushed back to shore, and handed him to the two officers. He headed back to the chunk of ice, knowing the two officers would start mouth to mouth resuscitation immediately.

By this time the two other boys were freezing and frightened. When Cowger finally got to the ice, he put out a hand. The boys clung to their spots on the ice too frightened to move. "Come on," the officer reassured them. "We're going to be all right." He took one under one arm, assured the other boy that he would be right back, and headed for shore.

Minutes later, the three boys were on their way to the hospital. A worried Cowger asked one of the policemen how the boys were doing. The officer looked straight at Cowger before he answered. "The doctors at the hospital are taking care of them, but what about you?" Cowger was shaking from head to foot. He started to answer that he was all right, but the other officer grabbed a blanket and flung it over Cowger's shoulders. "I'm taking you to the hospital too."

Officer Cowger's temperature had dropped almost seven degrees, but the next day he was up and around—and worried about how the boys were doing. A few days later, when he got the word that the boys were all right, he breathed a deep sigh of relief. Like Officer Castellini, he was glad he had jumped right in, instead of waiting for more help, glad he had acted quickly. And glad—and proud—that his fellow officers had been there to help.

Writing/Journal Activities

1. THE STORY

Make up three good questions about this story. Write the answers after each question.

2. WHAT'S THE QUESTION?

Here are six questions a reporter might have asked one of the police officers in the story. Copy out what you consider the three most important questions.

1. "Why do you think you were awarded the Medal of Honor?"

2. "Were you in uniform when you rescued the driver of the auto?"

3. "Do you think a woman police officer could have done the same thing?"

4. "Did you realize how dangerous it was?"

5. "What kind of car were you driving?"

6. "How long is this freeway?"

3. FIND THE HEADLINE

Here are three newspaper headlines. Copy out the one headline that best tells the main idea of the story.

1. Police to the Rescue

2. Police Chase Ends in Crash

3. Police Officers Risk Lives to Save Others

4. SEARCH AND FIND

Find the word (or words) closest to the meaning of the underlined word in each sentence. Then copy the sentence, using that word (or words) in place of the underlined word.

1. Police departments present medals to officers for their <u>valor</u>.
   hard work   years of service   bravery   good discipline

2. The car smashed against the freeway <u>barrier</u>.
   sign   fence or wall   underpass   bridge

3. He heard the <u>screeching</u> noise.
   high pitched   growling   deafening   metallic

4. The officer <u>reassured</u> the man.
   yelled at   discouraged   warned   encouraged

5. The driver <u>pleaded</u> that the officer do something.
      begged   screamed   swore   demanded

6. The man could not be <u>budged</u>.
      awakened   overtaken   moved   frightened

Let's Talk—Discussion Activities

5. THINK IT THROUGH

Give as many answers as you can for each question.

— What are the main reasons people have for becoming police officers?

— Why is training considered so important?

— Why is experience also considered important?

— Why do you think police departments award the Medal of Valor each year?

6. TAKE A SIDE

Here are two opinions on the same subject. Take one side or the other, and then give all the reasons you can for the side you take.

—"Police officers need to be more understanding and agreeable when they deal with people."

—"People need to be more understanding and agreeable when they deal with police officers."

Cooperative Group Activities

7. IMAGINE

Imagine that you are in charge of selecting and training police officers. Pick the five most important qualities in this list that you would want an officer to have. There are no "right" or "wrong" answers, but be able to explain or justify your answers.

brave	honest	healthy	tall	understanding
experienced	young	patient	punctual	aggressive
intelligent	tenacious	friendly	generous	strong

8. LOOK BACK

Select one of the events shown on the timeline for this story. Use other books or articles to gather more information about the event, and try to find out why the event was important. Present the information to the class or group.

1993

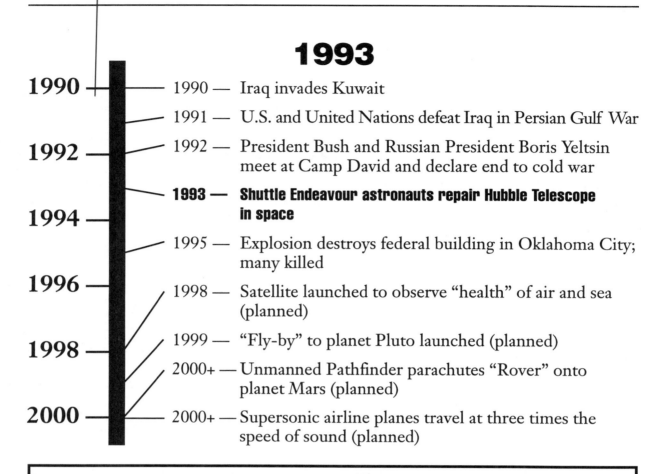

1990 — Iraq invades Kuwait

1991 — U.S. and United Nations defeat Iraq in Persian Gulf War

1992 — President Bush and Russian President Boris Yeltsin meet at Camp David and declare end to cold war

1993 — Shuttle Endeavour astronauts repair Hubble Telescope in space

1995 — Explosion destroys federal building in Oklahoma City; many killed

1998 — Satellite launched to observe "health" of air and sea (planned)

1999 — "Fly-by" to planet Pluto launched (planned)

2000+ — Unmanned Pathfinder parachutes "Rover" onto planet Mars (planned)

2000+ — Supersonic airline planes travel at three times the speed of sound (planned)

1990
1992
1994
1996
1998
2000

What Else Was Happening?

Iraq invaded the tiny country of Kuwait in 1990. The U.S. believed that Iraq was planning to attack other countries in the Middle East as well in order to gain control of the oil in that region. When Iraq refused to leave Kuwait, President Bush ordered hundreds of thousands of American troops to the Middle East. At President Bush's urging, other countries in the United Nations also sent soldiers to the area. After only four days fighting, Iraq was badly defeated and was forced to surrender.

Shortly after World War II ended in 1945, the United States and the Soviet Union began what came to be called the "cold war." Though the countries were not at war with each other, each country had large supplies of nuclear weapons aimed at each other. The two countries remained suspicious of one another, and the U.S. did all it could to stop the Soviet Union from spreading communism to other parts of the world. Finally, in 1990, the Soviet Union broke up into smaller countries. In 1992, Russia, the largest and most important of these countries, and the U.S. agreed to end the cold war that had lasted more than 45 years.

#15

A Rendezvous In Space

The scientist slumped uncomfortably at his desk at the space center and stared at the photographs in his hand. A worried expression settled on his face as he handed the photos to the scientist seated next to him. The second scientist looked at the photos, and shook his head. "These photographs—they're all blurred," he muttered.

American engineers and scientists had worked for many years designing and building a telescope the size of a bus. When completed, the telescope was loaded aboard a space shuttle and placed in orbit 365 miles above the Earth. Because it circled the Earth high above the Earth's atmosphere, the telescope was supposed to send back better and clearer pictures of distant parts of the universe—better and clearer than any telescope on Earth could do. At least that had been the hope of the scientists.

Now the first photographs were coming back—and they were all out of focus! What a terrible disappointment. Astronauts had risked their lives placing the Hubble Space Telescope (that is what it was called) in orbit. The project had cost two billion dollars. And now, so it seemed, all was lost. Everyone wondered: *what went wrong? why wasn't the telescope working? what could have happened?*

Scientists set about finding the answers to these questions. After careful study, the scientists were able to explain exactly why the Hubble Telescope was not taking good pictures. A mirror on the telescope had not been ground correctly—it was off by 1/50th of the width of a human hair! That is, it did not have the exact correct curve so that no matter what the scientists did on Earth, the pictures would come back out of focus. *But wasn't there some way or some thing that could be done to get the telescope to send sharper pictures back to Earth?* Yes, the scientists answered. If special lenses—curved exactly right—were placed inside the telescope, the mistake would be corrected. But that would take another astronaut space mission, one even more dangerous than the one that put the telescope in orbit. It would cost over six hundred million dollars. And, what's more, no matter how hard everyone worked, there was no guarantee that the telescope would work.

Why take such a chance?

The scientists listened to all the reasons for not going ahead.

Actually, they had planned to service the telescope on a regular basis anyway, but now the mission would be more difficult. Finally, they reached a decision: we will begin plans for a team of astronauts to service and repair

Astronaut Kathryn Thornton had good reason to feel confident about the mission.

stranger seeing Kathryn Thornton for the first time might have been a little surprised to learn she was an astronaut. She stood 5 feet 4 inches and weighed a scant 115 pounds—hardly an imposing looking figure. But anyone familiar with space flight knew that it took a lot more than strength to get the job done in a weightless space.

Astronaut Thornton felt confident about the mission—and with good reason. She was part of a team, and each member of the team was capable and experienced. Richard Covey was a veteran at repairing equipment in space; Jeffrey Hoffman was a physicist like her; Tom Akers, an experienced pilot and space walker; Claude Nicollier, a Swiss air force captain and astronomer; Story Musgrave, a medical doctor and a mathematician; and Kenneth Bowersox was an engineer and old hand Navy test pilot. Dr. Thornton knew she was in good company.

Shortly after being selected, the astronaut team began the most rigorous training program any group of astronauts had ever taken on. To simulate the weightlessness of space, they did their training in a tank filled with a million gallons of water. Every move, every action they would make in space had to be

the Hubble Space Telescope. A mission more dangerous, more complicated, and, yes, more daring than any mission since the walk on the moon 25 years before was set to begin...

Astronaut Kathryn Thornton was quite excited when she got word that she was one of the seven astronauts selected for the Hubble Repair Mission. She should not have been surprised. She had a doctor's degree in physics, and had already logged hundreds of hours in two earlier space flights. Yet, a rehearsed over and over. Every day, seven days a week, they practiced in bulky suits and huge, unwieldy, gloves that made the simplest movements difficult. For ten months, they pushed themselves...

On an early December morning in 1993, the seven astronauts climbed aboard the Space Shuttle Endeavour at the Kennedy Space Center in Florida. "Mission Specialist" Kathryn Thornton took her place. She listened as the countdown began. *Ten, nine, eight...* She knew that once the eight bolts that held the rocket ship in place were blasted away, and the Shuttle pushed skyward, there would be no room for mistakes—no turning back in case of error. Everything had to be done right. Still, she felt ready, eager, confident as the countdown continued. *Three, two, one—Blast Off!*

The "lift off" went perfectly. Two days later the Endeavor closed a 6700 mile gap, caught up with the Hubble Telescope, and then steered to within 35 feet of the telescope. A giant robot arm emerged, grabbed the four-story high telescope, and held it in place. Now, the most dangerous and complicated mission since the first moon landing would begin. Only Kathryn Thornton's bulky suit protected her from the deadly 300-degrees-below-zero temperature as she ventured into space atop the robot arm. Slowly, she eased the huge box containing the corrected lenses onto the telescope. Over the next two days, moving from the shuttle to the huge telescope in five separate trips, the astronauts put in new lenses, replaced a camera, added four huge solar panels, and repaired three faulty gyroscopes.

Eleven days after they had blasted off, the seven weary astronauts returned safely to Earth. The scientist were overjoyed. The Hubble would soon be sending sharp pictures back to Earth. What's more, the Endeavour mission had proved that men and women could make complicated repairs in space. This kind of know-how was necessary before a permanent station could be established in space. A giant step had been taken in America's efforts to conquer space.

Before the Endeavour's success, many Americans wondered whether or not to keep the space program going. Now scientists looked to future space journeys with a new optimism. American scientists, working with scientists from other countries, are setting goals for projects that will take them well into the twenty first century: an unmanned "flyby" to the planet Pluto; an unmanned trip to Mars that will parachute a "rover" robot to crawl over the surface of the planet; a satellite, called "Mission to Planet Earth" that will send back health information about the Earth's air and water. Despite these space plans, some Americans argue that it would be much better to spend the billions of dollars the space program costs on projects right here on earth. One thing is certain—the argument will continue well into the twenty first century.

Writing/Journal Activities

1. THE STORY

Make up three good questions about this story. Write the answers after each question.

2. WHAT'S THE QUESTION?

Here are six questions a reporter might have asked Dr. Kathryn Thornton after her mission. Copy out what you consider the three most important questions.

1. How did your education and training help you?
2. Why was the mission so important?
3. How tall are you?
4. What is the name of the robot arm used on this mission?
5. Who boarded the Endeavour first?
6. Why should we continue the space program?

3. FIND THE HEADLINE

Here are three newspaper headlines. Copy out the one headline that tells the main idea of the story.

1. Kathryn Thornton Selected for Space Journey Aboard the Endeavour
2. Hubble Telescope Mission Proves Repairs Can Be Made in Space
3. Astronauts Return After Eleven Day Journey in Space

4. SEARCH AND FIND

Find the word (or words) closest to the meaning of the underlined word in each sentence. Then copy the sentence, using that word (or words) in place of the underlined word.

1. The Hubble Space Telescope <u>orbits</u> the Earth.
   studies   circles   sends photos to   surveys
2. The first Hubble Space Telescope mission cost well over a <u>billion</u> dollars.
   ten thousand   ten million   a hundred million   a thousand million
3. Kathryn Thornton is an expert in the science of <u>physics</u>.
   animals   matter and energy   plants   gems and metals
4. The mission had a number of <u>veteran</u> astronauts.
   enthusiastic   new   experienced   eager
5. Each astronaut went through <u>rigorous</u> training.
   tough   expensive   under water   safe
6. The astronauts had to work with gloves that were <u>unwieldy</u>.
   hard to manage   uncomfortable   especially large   very loose